PATHWAY
TO
FREEDOM

PATHWAY TO FREEDOM

How God's Laws Guide Our Lives

ALISTAIR BEGG

MOODY PUBLISHERS
CHICAGO

Edited by Anne Scherich
Interior design: Ragont Design
Cover design: Erik M. Peterson
Cover photo of Bible copyright © 2014 by Gospel Perspective / Lightstock.
        All rights reserved.

Library of Congress Cataloging-in-Publication Data

Begg, Alistair.
    Pathway to freedom : how God's laws guide our lives / by Alistair Begg.
      p. cm.
    Includes bibliographical references.
    ISBN: 978-0-8024-1274-4
    1. Ten commandments. 2. Christian life. I. Title.

BV4655 .B384 2003
241.2'2—dc21

                                                                2002153829

We hope you enjoy this book from Moody Publishers. Our goal is to provide high-quality, thought-provoking books and products that connect truth to your real needs and challenges. For more information on other books and products written and produced from a biblical perspective, go to www.moodypublishers.com or write to:

Moody Publishers
820 N. LaSalle Boulevard
Chicago, IL 60610

1 3 5 7 9 10 8 6 4 2

Printed in the United States of America

To Cameron, Michelle, and Emily
"These commandments . . . are to be upon your hearts."
—Deuteronomy 6:6

To see the law by Christ fulfilled,
And hear His pardoning voice,
Changes a slave into a child,
And duty into choice.

—William Cowper
Love Constraining to Obedience

CONTENTS

FOREWORD

$\mathcal{T}$his book addresses a subject of critical and urgent importance. This past summer the National Association of Scholars released the report of their survey of a random sample of graduating seniors about what they had learned in college about ethics and morals in the workplace.

Nearly all the respondents said that college had prepared them ethically for their professional lives. At the same time, three quarters reported that they had been taught that "what is right and wrong depends on differences in individual values and cultural diversity." That is, they believe they are prepared ethically to live in a world where ethical behavior is purely circumstantial and can change from day to day.

Meanwhile, several years ago, their parents were polled and asked if they thought the Ten Commandments were relevant for living today. Two thirds of all Americans said they were and indeed they are; the Decalogue is the very foundation stone of Western law. Yet when asked to list the Ten Commandments—so relevant for living today—most people could not even name five. Dismal biblical ignorance.

We have entered into a time of moral crisis in our culture and the sad fact is that we have entered into a time of moral crisis in the church as well. Stories and statistics about divorce, adultery, lying, and the individualized picking and choosing of doctrines abound.

Into our confused world and church, one of the most gifted communicators I know, Alistair Begg, brings the one message which can give us order, direction, and hope. For the reader, he brings to life in the most readable way, God's commands, which God Himself wrote on the tablets Moses delivered to the covenant people.

Drawing on the Scriptures along with Puritan and other rich sources, Begg carefully helps the reader avoid the two great dangers associated with the Ten Commandments: legalism and license. He points out to the legalist that obedience to the Commandments is not the source of our justification or our sanctification. God does not love us more if we obey the Commandments and less if we do not. His love for us, our justification, our sanctification, and our final glorification were settled once and for all by the perfect faithfulness of Christ on the cross, not day by day by our grossly deficient faithfulness. Legalism is thus ruled out.

He goes on to point out the dangers of license, of ignoring the Commandments. After all some argue, we are beyond the law—beyond the Ten Commandments. Jesus commanded us to love God and love our neighbors. Isn't that enough? Hardly. Our sinful nature easily twists love into any shape that seems convenient to us at the time. And it is here that we desperately need moral direction from God, which He gives us in the Ten Commandments.

The Ten Commandments spell out what love for God and our neighbor looks like. The content of our love for God and neighbor is not for us to decide. We are too sinful, too selfish, and too foolish to make our own decisions about these matters. Without divine holiness, love, and wisdom we will go wrong, and the Holy Spirit, who superintended the writing of the Scriptures, uses the Ten Commandments to guide us.

This book had its genesis in a series of sermons about the Ten Commandments delivered to the congregation at Parkside Church where Alistair Begg serves as the much loved and respected senior minister. Though rich in exegetical insight and theological depth, this is not a book of exegesis or theology. While thoroughly scholarly, the book reflects the heart of its author. Alistair Begg is above all a pastor and a preacher—and a great one. As a result, this is a practical book for Christians who, out of love for the God who has saved us, sincerely want to walk in His ways and live out His will out of love for Him and our neighbors.

Pathway to Freedom is forthright and necessary teaching that today's church cannot afford to ignore. How now shall we live? The beginning of the answer must be: in obedience to God's moral law summarized in the Ten Commandments.

Charles W. Colson
Prison Fellowship Ministries
Washington, D.C.

PREFACE

*W*hen I preached a series of sermons on the Ten Commandments at Parkside Church in the fall of 1993, the response of the congregation was one of what might be called intrigued affirmation. They were, I think, largely caught off guard by an approach to the Moral Law which underscored its permanent validity in living the Christian life. For some, these commandments had never been considered since religion classes at parochial school. Others, brought up on an earlier diet of dispensationalism, had been taught that the Law belonged to another place and time and consequently had no pressing relevance. There were those whose political concerns caused them to be agitated by the removal of the Ten Commandments from public display. They were certain about the civil or political use of the Law but at the same time were at best confused about its function in their personal lives. In the goodness of God, by the time the series concluded, each of us in the congregation had a new appreciation for the words of the psalmist: "*The law of the* LORD *is perfect,* reviving the soul. The statutes of the LORD are trustworthy, making wise the simple. . . . By them is your servant warned; in keeping them there is great reward" (Psalm 19:7, 11, italics added).

When the series aired on the radio, once again there was a significant response. The largest mailbag came after the fourth commandment. This did not surprise me, because nothing illustrates the challenge in dealing with the abiding sanctity of God's Law more than the sorry state of the Lord's Day in contemporary evangelicalism. Actually, the biggest response was from Seventh Day Adventists, who wrote to correct me on what they regard as the mistaken notion that the Lord's Day should be celebrated on Sunday.

Given the response to these sermons, my friends at Moody Publishers persuaded me to turn the spoken word into the written word. This has proved to be a far harder task than any of us imagined. First, because although I write a full manuscript in preparing to preach, I write to speak and not to be read, and there is a considerable difference between the approaches. The second obstacle is related to the first. In preaching the series, I chose to tackle each commandment as a separate entity. I did not address important surrounding issues. However, when it came to the printed page, I could not ignore the inevitable questions arising in the mind of the reader. For example:

- The crucial relationship between Law and Love
- The place of the Law, since we are "not under Law"
- Our Lord's understanding and teaching of the Law
- The contemporary disregard for God's Law in both church and culture

• The age-old battle between legalism and license

The third obstacle was simply that I was unconvinced that this series of sermons would make any necessary and useful contribution to the significant number of helpful books on the Ten Commandments already in circulation. I was helped over this hurdle in reading Ernest Kevan's observation on the many voluminous expositions of the Moral Law that had come from the pens of the Puritans. Their value was found, "not so much in the substance of the expositions themselves, but in the underlying presupposition that the commandments are still obligatory."[1] They had no problem with the paradox that "only by obedience to the Law was the believer free from it."[2]

For the same reason then I hope that this book will prove helpful. I find my small voice absorbed in a vast chorus of those who throughout the ages have sung the psalmist's song: "Let me live that I may praise you, and may your laws sustain me" (Psalm 119:175).

Overcoming these obstacles has not happened without the help and encouragement of friends, colleagues, and family. My dear friend Sinclair Ferguson read the prologue and although he should not be found guilty by association, his kind insight was a great help. Robert Wolgemuth's friendship, encouragement, and guidance have made a vital contribution and I thank him.

Once again, I am grateful to Greg Thornton and all the team at Moody Publishers, who have with seasoned grace not simply tolerated all my fits and starts and stops but treated me with undeserved patience and grace.

I am immensely grateful to Judith Markham, who responded generously to my cry for help. Her ability in bridging the gap between the spoken and written word is so well known that my acknowledgement while being superfluous is nonetheless sincere. My assistant, Joy, has helped me immensely at every turn. Her ability is matched by her selflessness and I am ever thankful for her happy disposition.

To my colleagues and congregation at Parkside, without whose loyalty and love I would be completely at sea, my humble thanks. A special thank you to the elders at Parkside, who generously gave me sabbatical leave, making it possible for Susan and me to have time not only for rest and reflection but also to make possible the completion of this project. Paul and Betsy Seegott provided us with such a lovely place to relax and write, and we will not forget their generosity.

Without Susan's prayerful, kind, steadying, and encouraging influence, this project would have ended up in the file marked "unfinished business." For all the times she bit her tongue when she no doubt wanted to give me a much needed verbal "kick in the pants"; for not saying, "Do you know how long you have until this manuscript is due?" and for twenty-seven plus years of constancy, I thank her.

PROLOGUE

$\mathcal{E}$very well-taught English schoolboy knows that Admiral Lord Nelson defeated the combined French and Spanish fleets at the Battle of Trafalgar. Although mortally wounded by a French sharpshooter, Nelson was able to send a final signal from H.M.S. *Victory* to his navy. At 11:15 A.M. on the 21st of October 1805, just minutes before the commencement of the battle, this flag signal was raised on the mizzenmast:

> ENGLAND EXPECTS THAT
> EVERY MAN WILL DO HIS DUTY

And so in the performance of duty they pushed on to victory and bore testimony to the love of country that filled their hearts. Their motivation was love, but that love was defined by their obedience to command and the fulfillment of duty.

This simple illustration provides an immediate challenge, because, if we are prepared to be honest, we face the fact that in contemporary evangelicalism duty along with truth has fallen in our streets. The average church attendee has grown accustomed to responding to sermons that appeal to their sense of well-being. They are prepared to be coaxed but not to be commanded, particularly if the call to duty would prove a source of personal inconvenience. Neil Postman observed that effectiveness in TV preaching was in part tied to making sure that the preacher avoided making any demands upon his listeners.[1] This is sadly also true in the preaching of too many local churches.

The cultural climate is one in which there is plenty of room for personal preferences and little if any for eternal principles. Instead of the church seizing the opportunity to proclaim God's Law and sin as an offence against that Law, it is guilty of an embarrassing silence. Issuing God's people with a Nelsonian call to duty is regarded as the very last thing we require. This idea surfaces in sermons that begin by seeking to put the people at their ease. The preacher may begin, "I'm not going to preach, I just want to suggest some ideas for your consideration, and it is my sincere desire that you will all leave feeling much better about yourselves than when you arrived." With such a strategy there is little possibility of the listeners being "cut to the heart" and asking, "What shall we do?" as they did when Peter preached at Pentecost (Acts 2:37). From this perspective, Paul clearly missed the mark by confronting Felix and Drusilla with a discourse on righteousness, self-control, and the coming judgment! (Acts 24:25).

A negative reaction to the idea of "duty" is also prevalent in contemporary Christian literature. In the introduction to his book *Wild at Heart*, John Eldridge states that what men require is "permission to live from the heart and not from a list of 'should' and 'ought to' that has left so many of us tired and bored."[2] Perhaps the author is simply debunking a sterile moralism that has the "appearance of wisdom but which lacks any value in restraining sensual indulgence" (Colossians 2:23). But I wish he had not put it in those terms. He creates the impression that the "ought to" and the "should" of duty are antithetical to an adventuresome passion for God. But what God has joined together, namely law and love, no man should endeavor to pull apart. Jesus told His disciples: "If you love me, you will obey what I command" (John 14:15).

I remain unconvinced that the issues I and other men face are fatigue and boredom resulting from a call to arms. I am more inclined to believe that my problem is that I am fat and flabby and that Dr. J. I. Packer is right when he says, "Here then is the root cause of our moral flabbiness; we have neglected God's Law."[3]

In contrast to the confusion in contemporary Christianity about this matter of Christian duty, when we turn to the Shorter Catechism we discover a refreshing clarity. The Westminster Divines intended this brief compendium of theology as a teaching basis for an introduction to the Christian faith. Many of us have neglected to our impoverishment the concise summaries of faith provided in the Apostles' Creed and the Catechism. It is not too late to rectify the problem and to employ these supplemental aids to guide us on the journey. There is in the Shorter Catechism a logical progression that is as helpful as it is clear.

Question 1: What is the chief end of man?

This most basic question confronts each of us. Why am I here? What is the reason for my existence? What is the purpose of my life? The catechism on the basis of 1 Corinthians 10:31

and Psalm 73:25 provides the familiar answer. "Man's chief end is to glorify God, and to enjoy him forever."

Question 2: What rule has God given to direct us how we may glorify and enjoy Him?

We do not look within ourselves for the answer. Instead "The Word of God which is contained in the Scriptures of the Old and New Testaments, is the only rule to direct us how we may glorify and enjoy Him."

Question 3: What do the Scriptures principally teach?

"The Scriptures principally teach what man is to believe concerning God, and what duty God requires of man."

We then have to wait until Question 39 picks up the theme and further develops it:

Question 39: What is the duty which God requires of man?

"The duty which God requires of man, is obedience to His revealed will."

Instead of this leading to some kind of subjective quest whereby we attempt to discover the direction in which God is apparently moving and then join Him, the Westminster Divines send us straight to the Bible itself. They were convinced of the absolute sufficiency of the Word of God. We also need to be convinced! Three hundred years later, Professor John Murray expressed the same conviction. "There is no circumstance or situation in life in all its variety and detail for which the revelation of God's will in inspired Scripture is not a sufficient guide."[4]

Question 40: What did God at first reveal to man for the rule of his obedience?

"The rule which God at first revealed to man for his obedience, was the moral law."

Question 41: Where is the moral law summarily comprehended?

"The moral law is summarily comprehended in the ten commandments."

It is at just this point that confusion and division are apparent among God's people. Those of us who grew up relying too heavily on our *Scofield Reference* or *Ryrie Study Bible* have been led to believe that since we now live in the age of the church and await the age of the kingdom, the Law has no place in our lives. Again Murray, referring to the catechism's answer to Question 41 that we find our rule of life in the commandments, writes:

> *The statement of such a position is exceedingly distasteful to many phases of modern thought both within and without the evangelical family. It is agreed that the conception of an externally revealed and imposed code of duty, norm of right feeling, thought and conduct, is entirely out of accord with the liberty and spontaneity of the Christian life. We are told that conformity to the will of God must come from within and therefore any stipulation or prescription from without in the form of well-defined precepts is wholly alien to the spirit of the gospel. It is inconsistent, they say, with the spirit or principle of love: "Don't speak of law, nor of moral precepts, nor of a code of morals. Speak of the law of love."*[5]

Decades later, we may feel that his words fell largely upon deaf ears. Viewing the landscape of contemporary evangelicalism can it be doubted that the signs have multiplied that we neither know nor care much about the law of our God.[6]

- An absence of a true and realistic understanding of the seriousness of sin.
- Superficial preaching that appeals to man's felt needs and affection.

- A general listlessness and lawlessness in the lives of professing Christians.
- An absence of the fear of God in public worship and private living.
- A wholesale capitulation to the culture on the matter of the Lord's Day.
- Churches relying on strategies borrowed from business and psychology.
- A growing confidence in ourselves and an accompanying loss of confidence in God and His Word.

Martin Luther encouraged all who fear God, especially those who intend to become ministers of the gospel, to learn from the apostle Paul the proper use of the Law.

> *I fear that after our time the right handling of the Law will become a lost art. Even now, although we continually explain the separate functions of the Law and the Gospel, we have those among us who do not understand how the Law should be used. What will it be like when we are dead and gone?*[7]

It is time then for the lost art to be rediscovered.

Although the focus of this book is on the place of the Law in the life of the Christian, failure to give consideration to the place of law in the courts and culture would be a significant omission.

THE POWER OF GOD'S WORD

If you were given the opportunity to address seven hundred and fifty members of the legal profession, what would you say? One of the members of Parkside Church was receiving an award for outstanding work as a lawyer. He was given the opportunity of inviting two individuals to address the gathering. He graciously invited me, as his pastor, to address the company of his peers. Resisting every temptation to lead with my favorite lawyer story, I decided that I could do no better than read the Bible. Over the buzz of general conversation and the sounds accompanying the arrival of dessert, I began to read from the nineteenth psalm.

> The law of the LORD is perfect,
>> reviving the soul.
> The statutes of the LORD are trustworthy,
>> making wise the simple.
> The precepts of the LORD are right,
>> giving joy to the heart.
> The commands of the LORD are radiant,
>> giving light to the eyes.
> The fear of the LORD is pure,
>> enduring forever.
> The ordinances of the LORD are sure
>> and altogether righteous.
>
> —PSALM 19:7–9

Now I am well used to the public reading of Scripture and of doing so in the context of respectful silence. But on that day in the ballroom of the Renaissance Hotel, it was a different silence. So different that I can think of no other occasion I have experienced when the plain and straightforward reading of Scripture was accompanied by an almost palpable impact on all who were listening, myself included.

As I drove away from the city, I thought about the encounter that had taken place between the lawyers and God's Law. It bore testimony to the Word being sharper than a two-edged sword. On further reflection I wonder whether the assembly of lawyers was not dramatically impacted by the majesty of the Law of God as it is set out in Scripture. Not a few of those present would be quite prepared to admit that the grand ideas of truth and justice which had drawn them to a career in law had been lost along the way. They had been swallowed up in a system of plea bargains, out of court settlements, and the interminable juggling of conflicting agendas. The concept of an objective, valid standard of moral rectitude forming the basis for trial and judgment had been misplaced and neglected in the pressure to get a verdict.

So when they heard the Nineteenth Psalm ringing out in that lunchtime gathering, I am inclined to believe, that at least for some, there was a flicker of acknowledgment that in these timeless words we discover the foundation of law itself. The sense of disillusionment, skepticism, and ultimately cynicism that adheres to the practice and process of law can be traced to the crumbling confidence and, in some quarters, total disdain for the concept of God's Law. Chuck Colson quotes part of a speech given in 1979 by the late Arthur Leff of Yale Law School: "Unless there is a God who is Himself goodness and justice, there can be no ultimate moral basis for the law. For if there is no God, nothing can take His place. No human standard—no person, no group of people, no document is immune to challenge."[8]

This is not a remote discussion that can be safely left in the marble halls of justice or the ivory towers of learning; it is a matter of pressing urgency. Our views on issues like abortion, marriage, stem cell research, and homosexuality are tied directly to our convictions about the Moral Law. We understand the Moral Law to be an expression of the moral nature of God. This Law is transcendent and universal. Every person is dependent upon God and is responsible to God, and as hard as they may try to deny it, they have at least a sneaking suspicion that this is true. We are not surprised because God, as we are about to see, has engraved a sense of right and wrong in man's conscience.

If we are going to engage our friends in conversation on this subject, we need to realize how radically different our view of the world is from that of our secular neighbors. We have already noted that the Shorter Catechism tells us that God has given man His Moral Law for the rule of his obedience. But what do we mean by the giving of the Moral Law?

Paul refers to this when he writes in Romans 2 of the Gentiles who, although they are not the recipients of the Ten Commandments, "do by nature things required by the law," and in doing so, they "show that the requirements of the law are written on their hearts" (Romans 2:14–15).

Although men and women may be ignorant of the Law of God as it is revealed in Scripture, they have a law in themselves; their consciences confirm the fact of natural law. We know that there is a difference between right and wrong. Our consciences tell us so. But the question remains, How do we know what is right? In the course of everyday conversation it is not uncommon to hear someone challenge the notion of an objective universal standard. "Who's to say what's right?" As we saw earlier, no human standard is immune to challenge. God's Moral Law alone determines correctly the issues of right and wrong.

This Law did not begin with the thundering of Sinai; it came to Adam in the garden. As Klooster puts it, "God put Adam to the test as he explicated this law in a specific command. The heart of the test was simply this: *Love me, Adam, by obeying me, and obey me by loving me.* Love has always been the summary of the law."[9]

The Moral Law, summarized in the Ten Commandments, has an abiding place in the Christian's life. In affirming this, one is quickly confronted by the question: What about the ceremonial and judicial laws God gave to Israel?

The Westminster Confession is once again clear and helpful on this point.

> *Besides this law, commonly called moral, God was pleased to give to the people of Israel, as a church under age, ceremonial laws containing several typical ordinances; partly of worship, prefiguring Christ, his graces, actions, sufferings and benefits; and partly holding forth various [instructions] of moral duties. All which ceremonial laws are now abrogated under the new testament. (xix.iii)*

And the judicial laws, which God gave to them as a political body, "expired together with the state of that people."

The liturgical, ceremonial, and civil laws were purposeful, necessary but temporary, in contrast to the moral law, which again in the words of the Confession,

> *doth forever bind all, as well justified persons as others, to the obedience thereof; and that not only in regard of the matter contained in it, but also in respect of the authority of God, the Creator, who gave it. Neither doth Christ in the Gospel any way dissolve, but rather much strengthen this obligation. (xix.v)*

But surely not! Hasn't Paul told us, "You are not under law, but under grace" (Romans 6:14)? Yes, He certainly has, and it is therefore vital that we discover just exactly what that means.

The Perfect Law that Gives Freedom

Helvellyn is probably the most popular peak in the Lake District of northern England. In its shadow the poet William Wordsworth "wandered lonely as a cloud." Although it only rises to a modest 3,100 feet, it remains a favorite for climbers and hill walkers. The most challenging and consequently most popular route of ascent is via Striding Edge—the most famous of the "Look, no hands!" edges. Danger lurks on both sides. For each walker the challenge is clear. Stay on the path or fall into either the Red Tarn or Nethermost Cove, the deep and fearful gullies that await the careless and the negligent. Memorial stones stand as silent reminders of those who lost their lives in the attempt.

I remember as a young man listening to a preacher who suggested that Striding Edge provides a wonderful illustration of what it means for the Christian to walk the narrow path of obedience to "the perfect law that gives freedom" (James 1:25). Failure to take that route would find us falling inevitably into one of the two deadly gullies of legalism or antinomianism. Perhaps the speaker had been reading the comments of A. R. Vidler: "The Church on earth has always, as it were, to walk on the razor edge between legalism and antinomianism, between taking the Law too seriously and not taking it seriously enough. It is not surprising that every Church tends to err in one direction or the other."[10]

Legalism makes too much of the Law and robs the believer of his freedom in Christ. The legalist's whole approach to God is wrong, believing as he does that salvation actually depends upon observing various laws and regulations. In the early church, the Judaizers taught that along with faith in Christ, the keeping of the Law of Moses was also necessary, because without this, they said, there could be no justification. In response, Paul wrote his letter to the Galatians as the great charter of Christian liberty. In it he reminds his readers of the gospel:

> We . . . know that a man is not justified by observing the law, but by faith in Jesus Christ. So we, too, have put our faith in Christ Jesus that we may be justified by faith in Christ and not by observing the law, because by observing the law no one will be justified.
> —GALATIANS 2:15–16

Antinomianism (*anti,* against; *nomos,* law; i.e., being against the law) sets aside the Law of God, believing that it no longer has any place in the lives of believers. If the legalist believes that the Law is the solution, then the antinomian blames the Law for his problems and seeks to be rid of any obligation to its demands.

John Stott has a characteristically concise and helpful description of this distinction: "Legalists fear the Law and are in bondage to it. Antinomians hate the Law and repudiate it."[11]

But these are not the only options open to us. We need not fall into either one of these deep gullies. Remember Striding Edge! There is this narrow way taken by the law-abiding free people who love the Law and reject both legalism and license. This is the paradox of Christian freedom captured by the verse:

Make me a captive, Lord,

And then I shall be free;

Force me to render up my sword,

And I shall conqueror be.

It is no surprise that the Christian's relationship to the Law has been a problem since New Testament times. In seeking to hold in tension obedience to the Law and freedom in the Spirit, it is easy to misunderstand and to be misunderstood. Even a cursory review of church history makes clear that learning how to balance the requirements of the Law and the liberty of the Spirit has proved to be one of the harder theological puzzles and has tested the wisest and deepest thinkers. That should be an encouragement to those of us who do not fall within that category! In this context, no statement has been of greater help to me than these words of the Puritan author, Samuel Bolton:

> *The law sends us to the Gospel, that we may be justified, and the Gospel sends us to the law again to enquire what is our duty in being justified.* [12]

The Law informs us of what God requires and the Spirit empowers us as we fulfill our duty. At this point we must return to the question we have posed but left unanswered: What does the apostle mean when he declares, "You are not under law, but under grace" (Romans 6:14)? In what sense is it true to say that the believer is no longer under law?

The Christian Is Not Under Law as a Way of Justification

Paul makes this perfectly clear in Galatians 3:11. "Clearly no one is justified before God by the law." One way of testing whether we have a solid experiential grasp of this essential Christian doctrine is to determine how we react to the accusations of the Evil One. When he tempts us to despair and reminds us of our guilt, do we respond by pointing out our obedience and good deeds and righteous acts? I hope not. The only safe and true reaction is to point away to Christ and His having become a curse for us (Galatians 3:13). As Donald MacLeod puts it: "The law no longer has the authority to accuse the child of God or to instill in his heart the fear of final condemnation."[13] The Christian has been saved from sin's guilt, not by his obedience to the Law, but by the precious blood of Christ. He is, in A. M. Toplady's words, "a debtor to mercy alone." It was this amazing truth, which finally turned on the light for that earnest, devout, Roman Catholic monk, Martin Luther. Failing to find peace in his meticulous, rigorous observance of the Law, it finally dawned upon him that Christ had borne the curse in his place and that even though he was a Law breaker, Christ had kept the Law for him and he was justified by faith alone.

THE CHRISTIAN IS NOT UNDER LAW AS IT RELATES TO MOSAIC LEGISLATION

As we saw earlier, there was a strong movement in the early church to impose upon believers all the rules and regulations of the ceremonial and judicial law. When Paul called the Galatian believers to "stand fast in the liberty by which Christ has made us free" (5:1 NKJV), it was in the context of refuting those who were cutting in on these young Christians and trying to trip them up with the outward demands and signs of the Law. This is the key to understanding Paul's exhortation to the believers in Colossae regarding dietary rules and religious festivals. He is clearly *not* setting aside the Moral Law. He is pointing out that the ceremonial aspects of Judaism no longer have any hold on the Christian.

The Christian Is Not Under
Law as the Dynamic of Sanctification

Writing to the Galatians about life in the Spirit, Paul says, "If you are led by the Spirit, you are not under law" (5:18). In other words, we say no to sin and yes to righteousness, not as a result of struggling to keep the Law, but by the power of the indwelling Spirit. The Christian's motivation does not come from the Law. That is not to deny that some Christians are living their lives driven by a servile fear, which causes them to comply with God's requirements. But that is not how it is supposed to be. It is, as we understand God's love to us in Christ, that we find ourselves delighting in God's Law written in our hearts.

The antinomian reacts to this by suggesting that when the Law has sent us to Christ for justification, Jesus sends us not back to the Law but to the Spirit.

"Now," they say, "we live free from any consideration of those Old Testament laws, which only hinder and instead we breathe the fresh air of the New Testament emphasis upon love. After all, did not Jesus say, 'A new commandment I give you'"?

But it should be clear that Jesus was not setting aside the Moral Law and declaring that it was now irrelevant for His followers. "What is *new* about this is not the demand for love to one's brother, on which the Old Testament has a good deal to say, but the standard of love that Christ sets; the commandment is *new* simply because the love of Christ dying to redeem the ungodly creates an entirely new ideal of what mutual care and service among Christians ought to mean."[14]

Elsewhere Jesus makes clear to His followers that far from setting the Law aside, He is establishing it, underscoring its abiding relevance and application. "Do not think that I have come to abolish the Law or the prophets; I have not come to abolish them but to fulfill them" (Matthew 5:17).

Jesus rebuked the Pharisees: "You have let go of the commands of God and are holding on to the traditions of men" (Mark 7:8). This is not an unfamiliar pattern in many of our local churches. *Ironically, legalism seems to breed best where the Law of God is regarded as having no abiding place as a rule of life in the child of God.* The believer is then hedged about by man-made restrictions and taboos, what Paul refers to as "those weak and miserable principles" (Galatians 4:9). If we are to be safeguarded from falling into this gully, we must pay careful attention to what Jesus had to say about the Law.

When the expert in the Law tested Jesus by asking which of the commandments was the greatest, Jesus replied with two. "'Love the Lord your God with all your heart and with all your soul and with all your mind.' This is the first and greatest commandment. And the second is like it: 'Love your neighbor as yourself'" (Matthew 22:37–39). These verses are often used to justify the notion that somehow along the way the Ten Commandments of the Old Testament have been reduced to just two in the New. This is to ignore the clinching statement that Jesus went on to make: "All the Law and the Prophets hang on these two commandments." In other words, what Jesus has just provided is a summary of the summary (the Decalogue). The first table of the Law expounds what it means to love God; and the second, what it means to love our neighbor.

As Jesus' followers, we are not left to try and work out on our own what love will look like. For the Law is "guidance in loving." David Atkinson, in his commentary on Ruth, makes the point that Boaz was a law-abiding person: "For him Law is not a legal code only, it is a reminder that he is part of the family of the covenant God. Law for Boaz is fatherly instruction from God, not a moralistic legal code."[15]

We will return to this critical relationship between Law and Love. We will see that the Bible holds them together. They are like the wings of a plane. Both are equally necessary for flight. Love left to itself can so easily degenerate into sentimentalism. Law by itself quickly becomes legalism. I have a strange picture in mind. A runway filled with one-winged planes, which are going nowhere. Could it be a metaphor for too many Christians who are taxiing continually, unable to soar as God intends, in large measure because they fail to understand the critical relationship between Law and Love?

The idea that the Law has been abolished for Christians is alive and well at the dawn of the 21st century. Those holding this position teach that the only absolute left is the commandment of love. In seeking to steer clear of this deep, dangerous gully called antinomianism, those of us who affirm the permanent authority and sanctity of the Moral Law must remain vigilant lest in avoiding one gully we fall off "Striding Edge" into the other deep, dark hole called legalism. So before examining each of the commandments in turn, we must make sure that we understand the place and purpose of the Law that gives freedom.

During the British coronation ceremony in 1953, Queen Elizabeth II was presented with a Bible with these words:

> We present you with this Book, the most valuable thing this world affords. Here is wisdom. This is the Royal Law. These are the lively oracles of God.

The presentation provided a timely and necessary reminder to both the monarch and the people that the ultimate throne is God's and that the Law of God binds Her Majesty's Government.

THREEFOLD USE OF THE LAW

It is customary in theology to distinguish a three-fold use of the law.[16]

1. The Civil or Political Function of the Law

Even a superficial historical survey reveals the fact that the legal systems of both the United States and Great Britain begin with the conviction that there is a transcendent principle of right (natural law) to which all people are subject. In the United States, "liberty and justice for all" was a consequence of being a nation, UNDER GOD, we might say, under God's Law. But when the ship of state breaks its moorings at this point, then confusion and corruption is bound to follow. When we move "from God's standard to considerations of mere social convenience, the inevitable outcome will be laws which degrade and dehumanize."[17]

When the Supreme Court of the United States rendered its watershed decision in *Roe v. Wade* it had overstepped its legitimate authority. It possesses no right to enact laws on the basis of social utility divorced from absolute divine norms. If it had rendered a decision on the basis of God's moral law, then the court would have been forced to recognize that the sixth commandment which forbids murder takes precedence over any rights a woman may have in the matter of sexual freedom and the jurisdiction of her body.

In 1936 when the late Professor Gresham Machen delivered a series of radio talks on a Christian worldview, he argued that the only remedy for society's progressive decay was the "rediscovery of the Law of God." He was aware that his perspective was not the majority view: "I know that some of my hearers regard what I have been saying as being no more worthy of consideration than the hobgoblins and bogies with which nurses used to frighten naughty children."[18]

What would he think of our current brand of chaos where the courts function, "as little more than traffic cops, keeping people from bumping into each other as they do their own thing"?[19] God's Law exists in this civil realm to restrain wrongdoing and to promote right living.

Those of who grew up in the sixties were familiar with the hippie mantra, "All you need is love." This love was supposed to be an all-embracing tide, which we were told would pick us up and propel us into a new era of harmony and peace. But selfishness won the day. The times were changing and the folk heroes issued a warning to mothers and fathers all over the land not to criticize what they did not understand and to face the fact that their sons and their daughters were beyond their command and that their own road was now a road less traveled. After all, who would want to return to the enslavement of biblical ethics? We were told, for example, that outside the bonds of Christian marriage people would discover for the first time what true love is all about. The social history of the last four decades does not confirm the accuracy of the assertion. "People tend to imagine that the moment we move away from biblically controlled legislation we will get more freedom and more tolerance. That is not the lesson of history. What we will get is more inhumanity, more barbarism and more savagery."[20]

Is the situation then to be regarded as hopeless? Shall we throw in the towel and head for the hills to await the return of Christ? Absolutely not! The prospect of the return of Him who " is the end of the law" (Romans 10:4) should stir us to work while it is day. The post-9/11 philosophical and spiritual vacuum provides a unique opportunity for Christians to argue convincingly for a biblical worldview. We cannot do so effectively without addressing the absolute standard of God's moral law. In this task of effective, sensible, gracious, imaginative apologetics seldom has so much been left to so few!

Sadly the Christian witness is too often just like the average English speaker in a foreign country who is confident that he will be understood if he just speaks a little louder! So much of the moral dialogue and debate in the last twenty-five years has been an illustration of this ineffective strategy. If we are to correct our mistakes, it will demand humility and civility. Learning to engage our neighbors in conversation, listening to their view of the world, probing their arguments, and gently pointing out the logical implications of their views. We should be unashamed in affirming the validity and necessity of God's Law. After all, the alternative of unlimited personal freedom combined with a runaway materialism is producing an unsatisfied hunger and a dreadful loneliness. God's Law provides the foundation and parameters for civil and political freedom. Here we find timeless wisdom that is to regulate the daily discourse and which gives significance and purpose to life and work.

We must be prepared to affirm by lip and life, celibacy prior to marriage and monogamy within it. As we remind parents and employers that at home and work "honesty is the best policy," we build a bridge from a consideration of the Law to an introduction to the Lawgiver Himself. Luther reminded his community that the civil restraint imposed by God's Law was "intended by God for the preservation of all things, particularly for the good of the Gospel that it should not be hindered too much by the tumult of the wicked."[21]

Faced with this daunting task, we need to be encouraged. Here, again, is Machen:

*Do not fear you Christian. The Spirit of God has not lost His
power. In His own good time, He will send His messengers,
even to a wicked and adulterous and careless generation. He
will cause Mount Sinai to overhang and shoot forth flames. He
will convict men of sin; He will break down men's pride; He
will melt their stony hearts. Then, He will lead them to the
Savior of their souls.*[22]

2. The Pedagogical Function of the Law

Drawing on Paul's language in Galatians 3:24, the Reformers spoke about the pedagogical function of the Law.
The pedagogus in Roman culture was the slave who took
the child to school. So with Christ as the teacher, the Law
performs the function of leading the child to Him. Luther
referred to this as "the principle purpose of the Law and its
most valuable contribution." His statement to this effect is
so powerful that it is worth quoting it in its entirety.

*As long as a person is not a murderer, adulterer, thief, he would
swear that he is righteous. How is God going to humble such a
person except by Law? The Law is the hammer of death, the
thunder of hell and the thunder of God's wrath to bring down
the proud and shameless hypocrites. When the Law was instituted on Mount Sinai it was accompanied by lightning, by
storms, by the sound of trumpets, to tear to pieces that monster
called self-righteousness. As long as a person thinks he is right
he is going to be incomprehensibly proud and presumptuous.
He is going to hate God, despise His grace and mercy, and ignore the promises in Christ. The Gospel of the free forgiveness
of sins through Christ will never appeal to the self-righteous.
This monster of self-righteousness, this stiff-necked beast,
needs a big axe. And that is what the Law is, a big axe.*

Accordingly the proper use and function of the Law is to threaten until the conscience is scared stiff.[23]

Can you imagine Martin Luther speaking at one of the "ruffle no feathers" evangelistic services in many of our churches? Congregations that have grown accustomed to being treated with due deference; cajoled and appealed to by our seeker-driven talks would either be ramrod straight in their seats or running for the exits.

Are we prepared to consider the possibility (or as Luther would probably say, face the fact!) that much of our methodology owes more to the world of business and marketing than it does to the pattern of apostolic preaching so clearly displayed in the practice of the Reformers?

David Wells bemoans the situation within the evangelical church, "With its endless chatter about the self, its psychobabble, its easy gospel that asks for no repentance, its quick decisions that ask for no seriousness, its emptied out understanding of the necessity of Christ's death."[24]

Having discovered that Luther is correct in saying that the gospel of a free forgiveness does not appeal to the self righteous, we have with relative ease decided not to reach for the axe of the Law but instead have manufactured a "gospel" that *will* appeal. Tragically in most cases there is a failure on the part of preacher and people to recognize that this is "another gospel" which is actually no gospel at all (Galatians 1:7).

Calvin used a gentler picture when he described the Law as a mirror showing up the spots on our faces and sending us to Christ for cleansing.

So whether as an axe to threaten or a mirror to confront, this evangelical function of the Law serves to convict us of sin and convince us of our need of mercy and graciously lead us like a child to the free forgiveness of sins through Christ.

We will return to this function of the Law in the Postscript.

3. A Rule of Life for Believers

Ralph Erskine, the eighteenth-century Scottish preacher summarized the link between the second and third uses of the Law, in this way:

> *When once the fiery Law of God*
>
> *Has chas'd me to the Gospel Road;*
>
> *Then back unto the holy law*
>
> *Most kindly Gospel-grace will draw.*[25]

This expresses in quaint poetry the same principle we noted earlier in the words of Samuel Bolton: "The Gospel sends us to the Law again to enquire what is our duty in being justified."[26]

In affirming this third use of the Law, it is imperative that we are absolutely clear that the believer is free from the Law as a means of justification. He is not justified by keeping the Law, but having been justified, he keeps the Law. When the mirror of the Law is held before us and we are made aware of our sinful condition before God, we come to Christ, declaring with Augustus Toplady,

> *Not the labors of my hands*
>
> *Could fulfill Thy law's demands;*
>
> *Could my zeal no respite know,*
>
> *Could my tears forever flow,*

All for sin could not atone;

Thou must save, and Thou alone.

"But when we arise from our prostration before the cross, it is not to find the moral law abrogated, but to find it by the grace of God wrought into the very fiber of the new life in Christ. If the cross of Christ does not fulfill in us the passion of righteousness, we have misinterpreted the whole scheme of divine redemption."[27]

Calvin regarded this third use of the Law as the principal use.

> *The third and principal use, which pertains more closely to the proper purpose of the law, finds its place among believers in whose hearts the Spirit of God already lives and reigns. For even though they have the law written and engraved upon their hearts by the finger of God [Jeremiah 31:33; Hebrews 10:16], that is, have been so moved and quickened through the directing of the Spirit that they long to obey God, they still profit by the law.* (Institutes, 2.7.12)[28]

By means of the Law, the believer, Calvin taught, learns thoroughly the nature of God's will and he is aroused to obedience and drawn back from the slippery path of transgression.

Those who reject the permanent validity of the Law often base their objection on the idea that Love replaces Law in the living of the Christian life. The Christian, they say, is ruled by the spirit of Love and so is free from the Law as a rule of life. They reject the idea of the believer being guided and taught by the Spirit to display his love for God by keeping the commandments. Instead, they say, he lives, not by rules, but according to the judgments of his own heart as constrained by love alone.

Thomas Taylor challenges those who say that we must not live by any rules but simply in response to the "spiritual" promptings of the moment: "To say, we obey God by the spirit without a law or a commandment, is a mere pretence: for is any obedience without a law? What can be more ridiculous than for a subject to profess obedience to his Prince, but yet will not be under any law?"[29]

To substitute the judgments of our own hearts for the Law was, wrote Anthony Burgess in 1646, "to have the sun follow the clock."

The Puritans spoke about the believer keeping the law from an "evangelical ability." They understood that it is possible to "keep" the law externally and fastidiously in a form of moralism. In direct contrast, they realized that God has, if you like, fashioned the believer's heart in the shape of His Law so that he keeps the law not by natural endeavor but as a result of the energizing power of the Holy Spirit. He is working out his own salvation with fear and trembling NOT *in order that* BUT *because,* "it is God who works in you to will and to act according to his good purpose" (Philippians 2:13).

The Westminster Confession puts it this way: "The Spirit of Christ [subdues] and [enables] the will of man to do that freely, and cheerfully, which the will of God, revealed in the law, requires to be done" (xix.vii). This is not to be bound and restricted but to live in the freedom that the psalmist declared: "I will always obey your law, for ever and ever. I will walk about in freedom, for I have sought out your precepts" (Psalm 119:44–45).

God gave the Ten Commandments, not to the surrounding nations, but to His people. And they were laws for His redeemed people. "The great thing is that God did not take them out of the land of Egypt *because* they kept the Ten Commandments: they were to keep the Ten Commandments because God took them out."[30] In the same way, the Sermon on the Mount is delivered by Jesus, not as guide to *becoming* His disciple, but as a handbook for those who by God's grace *are* His disciples.

The Puritans believed that the highest spirituality was to be seen in a life that rejoices to be commanded. Now there is a concept that we do well to ponder! "It is no infringement to our liberty in Christ, to be tied to the performance of duty."[31] The command of the Law and the constraining power of Christ's love thus work in tandem to define the way in which the believer walks. Christians discover in Samuel Rutherford's memorable words: "The Law of God, honeyed with the love of Christ, has a majesty and power to keep from sin."[32] Or in the words of John Owen, "a universal respect to all God's commandments is the only preservative from shame."[33] Thus as the believer makes his journey to the Heavenly City, he must resist the libertine notions of Formalist and Hypocrisy and stand with Christian as he declares: "I walk by the Rule of my Master, you walk by the rude working of your fancies."

Perhaps Bunyan wrote those lines with Hebrews 10:16 in mind: "This is the covenant I will make with them after that time, says the Lord. I will put my laws in their hearts, and I will write them on their minds."

The writer of Hebrews is quoting from the promise of God in Jeremiah 31:31–34. Jesus has offered for all time one sacrifice for sin. The believer has been redeemed and set apart from a common to a holy use. Paul referred to this in 1 Corinthians 6:20. Since the believer has been bought at a price, he or she is to glorify God in their body. In affirming the fact that in the death of Christ, all that God wants has been achieved and all that we need has been accomplished, the Holy Spirit then testifies to the abiding place of the Law in the life of the believer. "By one sacrifice he has made perfect forever those who are being made holy." The believer has been changed inwardly, given a new heart, the same shape as the Law of God. It is a perfect fit. There is nothing irksome or uncomfortable about it. There is no conflict between that heart and the requirements of holy living. We make progress into a life of obedience to God's Law (Romans 6:13). How striking that the work of regeneration is here defined in terms of the Law being written on the heart and mind of the believer. As we heed the warnings and rest upon the promises of Scripture, the Holy Spirit works in our lives a supernatural principle which cannot be *acquired* by fulfilling our duties but it is *preserved* by them.

We have I hope covered enough ground to understand why it is that in every generation the church is tempted to fall into the gully of either legalism or license. Thirty years ago I remember sitting in church listening to the pastor rearrange the words of a well-known Easter hymn. The verse he changed reads as follows in its original form. "O dearly, dearly has He loved and we must love Him too. And trust in His redeeming love and try His works to do." The pastor suggested that we would be better served by changing the final phrase to read: "And trust in His redeeming love, *not* try his works to do." He presumably was seeking to counteract a view of Christian living that was marked by "slavish exertion." But in doing so he ran the risk of not getting the pendulum back to the middle, but of sending it to the other extreme; of suggesting a form of passivity that fails to reckon with Ezekial Hopkins' observation, "I much doubt, whether if God did not command us to do more than we can, we should do as much as we do."[34]

What he was suggesting was essentially the same as the assertion quoted earlier that we have "had enough" of being told that we need to be good and that what we need instead, is an adventure. Surely there can be no greater adventure than to live the Christian life, energized by God's Spirit and committed to an inward and spiritual obedience to God's Law. Such a wholehearted obedience is essential for us, since, in Robert Bolton's words, "He that endeavors not to be better, will by little and little grow worse."[35]

As we consider each of the Commandments in turn, we will, I think be helped, by keeping these three uses of the Law in mind. But having distinguished between them we will see the way in which all three uses function simultaneously in the Christian. For example when we consider the seventh commandment, we will see the importance of its civil function in preserving order in society. The Law will lead us afresh to Christ as we see our faces in the mirror and we will realize the Law's vital function as it rules on our behavior. It is imperative that we get this matter right. We dare not, as Luther reminds us, reject the Law altogether nor attribute to the Law a capacity to save.

> *There are three ways in which the Law may be abused.* First, *by the self-righteous hypocrites who fancy that they can be justified by the Law. Secondly, by those who claim that Christian liberty exempts a Christian from the observance of the Law. "These," says Peter, "use their liberty for a cloak of maliciousness," and bring the name of the Gospel into ill repute. Thirdly, the Law is abused by those who do not understand that the Law is meant to drive us to Christ. When the Law is properly used its value cannot be too highly appraised. It will take me to Christ every time.*[36]

THE TEN COMMANDMENTS

And God spoke all these words:

I am the LORD your God, who brought you out of Egypt, out of the land of slavery.

You shall have no other gods before me.

You shall not make for yourself an idol in the form of anything in heaven above or on the earth beneath or in the waters below. You shall not bow down to them or worship them; for I, the LORD your God, am a jealous God, punishing the children for the sin of the fathers to the third and fourth generation of those who hate me, but showing love to a thousand generations of those who love me and keep my commandments.

You shall not misuse the name of the LORD your God, for the LORD will not hold anyone guiltless who misuses his name.

Remember the Sabbath day by keeping it holy. Six days you shall labor and do all your work, but the seventh day is a Sabbath to the LORD your God. On it you shall not do any work, neither you, nor your son or daughter, nor your manservant or maidservant, nor your animals, nor the alien within your gates. For in six days the LORD made the heavens and the earth, the sea, and all that is in them, but he rested on the seventh day. Therefore the LORD blessed the Sabbath day and made it holy.

Honor your father and mother, so that you may live long in the land the LORD your God is giving you.

You shall not murder.

You shall not commit adultery.

You shall not steal.

You shall not give false testimony against your neighbor.

You shall not covet your neighbor's house. You shall not covet your neighbor's wife, or his manservant or maidservant, his ox or donkey, or anything that belongs to your neighbor.

—Exodus 20:1–17

1

NO
OTHER GODS

You shall have no other gods before me.
—EXODUS 20:3

$\mathscr{T}$wo religious convocations, one ancient and one modern, set the scene for our consideration of this first commandment.

In 1993 a parliament of the world's religions convened in Chicago. Seven hundred attendees sought common ground by minimizing their differences. They were in search of a multi-faith unifying consciousness. The mutual tapestry of understanding, respect, and cooperation, which marked the initial discussions, quickly unraveled as they began to tackle the substantial areas of disagreement. That event was separated from the ancient gathering by a few thousand miles and a few thousand years.

On Mount Carmel God's prophet Elijah went before the people and confronted them with their failure to give to God the loyalty He demanded and deserved. There was to be no attempt at blending the worship of Baal with the worship of Jehovah.

"How long will you waver between two opinions? If the
LORD is God, follow him; but if Baal is God, follow him."
—1 KINGS 18:21

Met with total silence, Elijah proposed "the battle of the
prophets." There were 450 prophets of Baal and on the op-
posing side, Elijah. If the numbers were any indication, it
would appear that the odds were heavily in favor of Baal.
The people were about to discover that one plus the living
God is a majority.

The terms of engagement were clear. The 450 would cut
a bull in pieces and put it on the wood. Then they would
call on the name of their god, imploring him to set fire to it.
Elijah would then do the same, calling on the name of the
Lord. Victory would be clearly established: The god who
answers by fire—He is God.

What followed was a scene that almost defies description. The prophets of Baal spent the entire morning wailing
and howling to no avail. Elijah's taunts hit them where it
hurt. Maybe their "god" was "deep in thought," in which
case it was pretty obvious that he wasn't thinking about
them. Maybe was "busy"—responding to a call of nature—
therefore, subject to human limitation. If he is "traveling"
and can't be present to help them, he is obviously not omni-
present. Perhaps he has grown weary and has fallen asleep,
and so they'll need to shout louder and awaken him. What a
picture of ecstatic frenzy as they pierce themselves and produce red blood but are totally unable to ignite red flames to
burn the bull. "There was no response, no one answered, no
on paid attention" (1 Kings 18:29).

In direct contrast and with ordered calm, Elijah repaired
the altar and had the offering doused three times with water.
God answered his prayer, and the people fell prostrate, pro-

claiming, "The LORD—he is God! The LORD—he is God!" (v. 39).

At issue was the question, Is there a God who hears prayer? The answer came with dramatic impact. Only one. *Yahweh.* He is the real God. In contrast, the gods of the nations are "nothing." The prophets Isaiah and Jeremiah seem to be constantly calling God's people away from the worthless foreign idols to the exclusive worship of the true and living God.

Their words do not fit the twenty-first century category of political correctness! Listen to Jeremiah: "For the customs of the peoples are worthless; . . . Like a scarecrow in a melon patch, their idols cannot speak; they must be carried because they cannot walk. Do not fear them; they can do no harm nor can they do any good" (Jeremiah 10:3, 5). In contrast, Yahweh declares, "There is no God apart from me, a righteous God and a Savior; there is none but me" (Isaiah 45:21).

God's demand for His people's total devotion is firmly based upon who He is and what He has done. He is both Creator and Redeemer. But why, the reader may be asking, have we launched immediately into this hotbed of debate? Should we not be facing up to our proneness to worship at the shrines of materialism, egotism, and intellectualism? Should we not begin by toppling some of these "gods" from the perches they occupy in our wayward hearts? True, each of us must face up to the peculiar personal temptation to idolatry, but it would be possible to do so and at the same time fail to be present where the battle rages. The Christian must resist the spirit of the world in the form it takes in his own generation. Is the epicenter of the storm really that obvious? I believe so.

In the 1960s, science, education, finance, arts, and the

media voted God out of office. No one wanted to hear from the "God-squad," and the prevailing mind-set was more than casual indifference towards God; it was willful disregard. The seeds planted in the 1960s blossomed in the 1970s and 1980s. But the quest for free love and unlimited self-expression issued not in beautiful foliage but in ugly weeds. Lawlessness, violence, and greed began to spoil and spread, as freedom, instead of being defined as the right to do what is right, became codified as the "unrestricted right to do whatever one pleases." As we careened toward the end of the millennium, Western culture was beset by a range of discontents and confusion. While the stock market took many to unimaginable heights of financial success, the culture was showing signs of futility, foolishness, and deep darkness. Drugs—made freely available to children at school. Perverted lifestyles—given the stamp of approval by the entertainment industry and of normality by segments of the church. Rap music—taking language to a new level of degradation, and young people working out their own damnation in the murder of their teachers and fellow students.

And so it appeared that Judge Bork was right when he said that we were "Slouching Towards Gomorrah."

Meanwhile, as the natural, scientific quest for utopia fizzled and materialism was yielding only greater hunger and lonelier heights, spirituality was waiting in the wings for a chance at the leading role. So there was hope, after all, we were told. We have come to the end of the age of disbelief, and as the new millennium beckons, perhaps the dawning of the age of Aquarius, about which the 1960s dreamed, was about to become reality. At least it was reckoned we were entering a new age of faith. In casual conversation, it was not difficult to get general agreement that as a society there would have to be more emphasis on responsibilities and less on our rights if we were going to pull out of what might be realistically seen as a moral and spiritual death spiral.

The frenzied greed, which had fueled the dot.com explosion, turned to wholesale panic as billions in value were flushed from the financial markets in less time than it had taken to accumulate. And then came the sad and horrific day at the dawn of this new millennium, 9/11/01, bringing many to their knees.

The "God is dead" slogan of the 1960s was to be replaced. "God is back," the newspapers declared, as countless individuals who had been quite content to live without any thought of God went in search of spiritual solace.

What a moment of opportunity! When Jesus saw the crowds, He was moved with compassion because He saw them as sheep without a shepherd. Responding as Christ did, we may declare Him to be the Good Shepherd who gives His life for the sheep. We must affirm that all who came before Him were thieves and robbers and that He alone is the gate that leads to the safety of forgiveness and eternal life.

Aye, but here's the rub. Surveys in this "new age of faith" reveal that more than three-fourths of all Americans believe that "many religions can lead to eternal life." Staggeringly, nearly half of those who identify themselves as "highly committed" evangelicals agree with this statement. The extent of the confused muddle-headedness on this matter within the ranks of professing evangelicalism is frightful but not surprising. Congregations that have been amassed without being instructed in basic Christian doctrine are devoid of the theological acumen and conviction necessary to hold firmly to the faith of our fathers.

It is here that the battle rages, and it is here that we must take our stand. Instead of mumbling some mushy religious pluralism, we need to be prepared to take our Bibles in hand and graciously, yet courageously, declare a worldview that begins with the God and Father of our Lord Jesus Christ, who in the person of His Son Jesus (with whom He and the Holy Spirit are co-equal and co-eternal) has stepped out of eternity and into time, demonstrating that He is neither anonymous nor vague.

> The grace of God that brings salvation has appeared to all men.
> —TITUS 2:11

The exclusive claims of the gospel are designed to reach all nations throughout the whole world. But if we are going to uphold this first commandment, we dare not flee from the battlefront at this point. Martin Luther said:

> *If I profess with the loudest voice and clearest exposition every portion of the truth of God except precisely that little point which the world and the devil are at that moment attacking, I am not confessing Christ, however boldly I may be professing Christ. Where the battle rages, there the loyalty of the soldier is proved, and to be steady on all the battlefield besides, is mere flight and disgrace if he flinches at this point.*

On the basis of this first commandment we must be prepared to declare that there is a decisive difference between the Christian faith and other religions. God is revealed in Scripture as powerful having spoken the world into being. He is perfect, self-existent, in need of no one and nothing. He is praiseworthy on account of His person and His works, and He is plural. He is *They.* Father, Son, and Holy Spirit. It is thus not possible for us to talk of God except in light of the unity that exists within the Trinity. The unity between Father and Son has clear implications for our reading of the first commandment. For example, how can Judaism claim to be worshiping God when they refuse to honor the Son?

> He who does not honor the Son does not honor the Father who has sent him.
>
> —JOHN 5:23

It is not arrogance that finds Christians making such declarations. Jesus is not simply a prophet standing on the same level as Muhammad. He is the incarnate God, and one day at the name of Jesus every knee, including that of Muhammad, will bow.

When we think this issue through, we realize why Paul describes the Ephesians before their conversion as living *without God.* Despite the fact that pagans can clearly be very religious (Acts 17 testifies to man's capacity to skillfully and imaginatively fashion idols for worship), that doesn't deny the necessity of their turning from their empty ways to the true and living God (Acts 14:15–16).

In stating these things, we must keep in mind that the warnings given by the prophets not to run after idols were directed not to the surrounding natives but to the people of God. The distinct contrast between the Christian faith and other religions should not be the basis of animosity or aversion toward non-Christians. In reaching our children about this we must affirm the importance of social tolerance. We must lead by example in treating our Hindu, Muslim, and Jewish neighbors and friends with genuine courtesy and respect. However, we must at the same time save our children from being swallowed up by a form of intellectual tolerance that fails to recognize the clear differences that exist between our Christian faith and the religions of our neighbors. For example, Hinduism says that God has been incarnated multiple times, but Christianity declares the Incarnation to be a unique event—we cannot both be right. Judaism says that Jesus was not the Messiah, but Christianity affirms that He is—again, we cannot both be right.

Of course, one of the peculiar challenges of our time is the rejection of the idea of universally valid truth. The collapse of scientific rationalism has paved the way for the idea that truth is what I reckon it to be. The huge change in the way people think about truth is humorously illustrated by Os Guinness, who tells the story of three baseball umpires discussing their profession.

> *The first umpire, who represents a traditional Christian view of the world, says, "There's balls and there's strikes, and I call them the way they are." In other words, he is saying, "There is such a thing as a ball and there is such a thing as a strike, and my job is to call them the way they actually are. The second umpire says, "No. No. There's balls and there's strikes and I call them the way I see them." This umpire says what's important is not whether or not it is a ball or a strike that comes over the plate, but what he sees. This relativistic view says that truth is what is true to me. In conversation with friends we find them saying—you have your truth, I have my truth. The underlying notion is that truth is what I perceive it to be and in the end all truths converge. The third umpire says, "No. No. No. There's balls and there's strikes and they ain't nothing till I call them." Balls and strikes don't even exist until he calls them into being by his own word. His radical perspective denies the idea of absolute truth.[1]*

It is not easy in this philosophical climate to hold firm to the biblical conviction that there is such a thing as truth and it is knowable and that when we say *God* it doesn't mean whatever we want it to mean. When Paul addressed the intelligentsia of Athens he was bold and unashamed: "The God who made the world and everything in it is the Lord of heaven and earth and does not live in temples made by hands. And he is not served by human hands, as if he needed anything, because he himself gives all men life and breath and everything else" (Acts 17:24–25).

Why was the city full of idols? Calvin writes of the way in which man makes for himself "shadow deities" so that he does not have to face the true God, whom he should reverence and adore. Paul explains in the first chapter of Romans that man is created with an awareness of divinity. Creation reinforces this awareness as we contemplate the order of the universe. Created to praise and worship the one true God, man suppresses the truth that is plain and invents for himself all kinds of pseudodeities. These are the sorry creations described by Isaiah as he pictures a man taking wood from the forest and with some of it lights a fire and with the rest of it fashions an idol.

> Half of the wood he burns in the fire;
>> over it he prepares his meal, . . .
> From the rest he makes a god, his idol;
>> he bows down to it and worships.
> He prays to it and says,
>> "Save me you are my god."
> They know nothing, they understand nothing;
>> their eyes are plastered over so they cannot see,
>> and their minds closed so they cannot understand.

No one stops to think,
    no one has the knowledge or understanding to say,
"Half of it I used for fuel;
    I even baked bread over its coals,
    I roasted meat and I ate.
Shall I make a detestable thing from what is left?
    Shall I bow down to a block of wood?"
He feeds on ashes, a deluded heart misleads him;
    he cannot save himself, or say,
    "Is not this thing in my right hand a lie?"
                —ISAIAH 44:16–20

As we have noted before, the prophet was not abusing the surrounding nations. Instead, he was confronting God's people with the amazing incongruity of their dilly-dallying with these "nothings" when their creator and redeemer called for their total devotion.

There is a sense in which the children of God are called continually to choose wisely and to ratify their choice in their lifestyle. **This first commandment excludes all the gods invented by men.** The Law of God is the lifestyle of the redeemed. His liberated people must not be foolish enough to go looking for the old gods beyond the river. This is the significance of the scene that comes at the end of the book of Joshua. Having summoned the leaders of Israel, this great general reminded them of how God had redeemed them and provided for them. Surely their hearts were so full of gratitude that they were shining examples of exclusive loyalty. Actually, no. Listen to what Joshua has to say:

Now fear the LORD and serve him with all faithfulness. Throw away the gods your forefathers worshiped beyond the River and in Egypt, and serve the LORD. But if serving the LORD seems undesirable to you, then choose for yourselves this day whom you will serve, whether the gods your forefathers served beyond the River, or the gods of the Amorites, in whose land you are living.

—JOSHUA 24:14–15

So Bob Dylan was right when he wrote the song, "Gotta Serve Somebody." Either the people of God will worship and serve the true and living God, or they must choose for themselves shadow deities for the object of their devotion.

The application of this historic incident is clear for the Christian. The liberation of God's people from Egypt foreshadows the even greater deliverance and redemption that is ours through the work of Christ upon the cross. The Christian's supreme loyalty is to the Lord Jesus, who loved him and gave Himself for him.

The point made so clearly in Joshua's call to the people is that to serve the living God means putting away other gods that are pretenders to the throne.

We make a grave mistake in assuming that because our houses are free of idols fashioned of metal, wood, or stone we have dealt with this and are ready to move on to the second commandment. The sobering truth to be faced up to is this: Anything or any person (including myself) that claims our primary loyalty has become "another God."

As we work our way through these commandments, we will constantly be on our guard against the spirit of the Pharisee, which contents itself with an outward conformity to the Law that is unmatched by the submission of the heart.

"Above all else guard your heart, for it is the wellspring of life." Solomon gives directions about our words and the gaze of our eyes and the path of our feet but the heart of the matter is the matter of the heart. Every idolatrous inclination begins in the heart.

—PROVERBS 4:23

While we are certainly not immune to the temptation to that which is clearly evil, the majority of our challenges will have to do with taking good things given for our enjoyment and devoting ourselves to them to such an extent that we make idols of them.

For example, let's take intelligence or academic success, physical fitness or sports and wealth as a reward for honest endeavor. We would be hard-pressed to argue against the benefit and enjoyment that are offered in these things. We recognize, as the Puritan Richard Sibbes said, "God has created worldly things to sweeten our passage into heaven."

Wisdom is described in Proverbs as being more precious than rubies. Paul tells Timothy that physical fitness has a certain value. Moses reminds the people that their ability to produce wealth is from the Lord.

The perversity of the human heart is such that even these good things may become the occasion of idolatry. In C. S. Lewis' *Screwtape Letters,* the devil instructs his understudy to encourage Christian to take these good things at the wrong time or in the wrong quantities. When that happens, the sweetness quickly turns sour. If we are not careful, wealth, wisdom, and strength quickly become grounds for boasting. So God issues this warning through His servant Jeremiah: "Let not the wise man boast of his wisdom or the strong man of his strength or the rich man of his riches, but let him who boasts boast about this: that he understands and knows me, that I am the LORD" (Jeremiah 9:23–24).

In a similar vein, Moses reminds the people of just how

crucial it is to "observe the commands of the LORD your God" and to reverence Him in their hearts as they walk in His ways (Deuteronomy 8:6). These commands would serve as an antidote to the temptation to forget the Creator because of a preoccupation with the creation. They were enjoying the "good life" on account of God's provision, and it was imperative that they did not lose focus. After enjoying a good meal, they should worship and praise God the giver. They should pay careful attention to all His commands, laws, and decrees. "Otherwise, when you eat and are satisfied, when you build fine houses and settle down, and when your herds and flocks grow large and your silver and gold increase and all you have is multiplied, then your heart will become proud and you will forget the LORD" (Deuteronomy 8:12–14).

Moses clearly did not believe that the people had no need of "the ought" and "the should" but instead required "an adventure." The blessings they enjoyed could so easily become the opportunity for the worship of self, and the people's propensity to pride needed to be harnessed by the reminder, "You shall have no other gods before me."

Each of us needs to come before God in a spirit of humility and be prepared to face up to the scrutiny we experience as we pray: "Search me, O God, and know my heart; . . . See if there is any offensive way in me" (Psalm 139:23–24).

I wonder if you have considered the possibility that some of our most precious earthly relationships can cause us to violate the first commandment. It is clear from the opening chapter of 1 Corinthians that Paul, Apollos, and Cephas had been granted a place in people's affections and loyalty that at least verged on idolatry.

Within the framework of marriage there is the distinct danger that a spouse may take first place in his or her partner's devotion. Have you never heard it said of a husband's loyalty to his wife, "He worships the ground she walks on"?

C. T. Studd recognized this tendency and wanted to prepare his wife for life without him. He encouraged her to remind herself routinely, "Lord Jesus, you are to me dearer than Charlie ever could be." The husband and wife will never find a greater mutual love than when urging each other to love the Lord with all their heart, soul, mind, and strength.

Dare we risk the scorn that may accompany the suggestion that our children may become idols? Again, is it not the case that a parent may be described as just "idolizing" his offspring? The family unit as a whole may actually become our focus when our focus should be on the Lord of the family. There is little doubt that family ties are the most frequent and acceptable excuses for disengaging from the gatherings of God's people in worship and the company of God's people in witness.

When we've been tempted to dismiss this idea as being un-Christlike, we do well to give careful thought to two brief scenarios in Luke's gospel, Luke 8:19–21 and 11:27–28. In each instance, Jesus places the hearing of and obedience to God's Word before considerations of family. The fact that this strikes us as so unbelievably strange is a further indication of the extent to which we have allowed the family to vie for that primary loyalty which belongs to God alone. He will not share His praise, which includes our loyalty, with anyone else. "I am the LORD; that is my name! I will not give my glory to another or my praise to idols" (Isaiah 42:8).

The series of sermons to which I referred earlier was titled *Guidelines for Freedom*. God demands our exclusive loyalty, and we find that in this complete devotion to the one God there is freedom. This is the freedom that comes from knowing that we are not held in the grip of blind forces or tossed about on the sea of chance but instead that in all things God is at work for the good of those who love Him. Surely providence is a soft pillow!

There is no limit to the benefits that we enjoy as we seek to remain faithful in our loyalty to the Lord. Even death does not bring an end to all that God has in store for those who love Him. The psalmist declares:

> You will show me the path of life;
> In Your presence is fullness of joy;
> At Your right hand are pleasures forevermore.
> —PSALM 16:11 NKJV

In conducting a wedding ceremony, I often urge the couple to ensure that they do not allow their eyes to wander, their minds to ponder, or their hearts to settle upon anyone or anything that will draw them away from each other. I have little doubt that on their wedding day they acknowledge my remarks, affirming them with every beat of their hearts. Such exclusive loyalty, if it is to be established over the long haul of married life, will demand from them sincerity, an unswerving focus, and a commitment to carefully maintain such devotion.

Christ loved the church and gave Himself up for her to make her holy. As His bride, the church is to keep herself from idols, to keep herself only unto Him. There can be no toying on the part of the bride with the seductive suggestions of pluralism or with the blatant advances of secularism. This commandment demands our exclusive and zealous worship. As individuals we must pay careful heed to the exhortation with which John ends his first letter: "Dear children, keep yourselves from idols" (1 John 5:21).

Such necessary vigilance demands that we are self-controlled and alert, for behind idolatry of every kind we will discover the deceitful scheming of the Evil One. In this endeavor we will be strengthened and renewed as we fix our eyes upon the Lord, "for only he will release my feet from the snare" (Psalm 25:15).

The dearest idol I have known,

Whate'er that idol be,

Help me to tear it from Thy throne,

And worship only Thee.

2
GRAVEN MISTAKES

You shall not make for yourself an idol in the form of anything in heaven above or on the earth beneath or in the waters below.

—EXODUS 20:4

*I*t is not uncommon for visitors to Parkside to comment on the plainness and simplicity of the room in which we meet to study the Bible and sing God's praise. Some are quite disturbed by the absence of "religious furniture" and certainly by the obvious lack of symbolism. Is the starkness of the setting because we have little appreciation for art and beauty? Hardly. Sculpture and paintings are gifts from God and are to be appreciated and enjoyed. Is the chaste simplicity merely representative of a style of interior design that is clean rather than cluttered? No. People are often surprised to learn that our structure reflects a theological principle and not an architectural preference. So, for example, the absence of any material altar is because Christ's once-for-all sacrifice of Himself is the only altar of the church in the New Testament (Hebrews 13:10). John Owen's observation on this verse is both timeless and timely: "The erection of any other altar in the church, or, the introduction of any other sacrifice requiring a material altar, is derogatory to the sacrifice of Christ, and exclusive of him from being our altar."[1]

Our design flowed from a desire to be free from distractions in seeking to worship God in spirit and in truth. This is in keeping with the second commandment, which teaches us to worship God in strict accordance with the manner in which He has revealed Himself to us. God alone is to be worshipped and without any visual symbols of Himself.

The first commandment arises by necessity on account of who God is and what He has done. In essence God says, "Because of who I am, Creator and Redeemer, nothing less than total devotion to me is in order" (see Exodus 20:3).

When we then proceed to ask, "How should I be a totally devoted person so as to keep the first commandment?" The answer is provided, says Alec Motyer, in the combined instruction of the second commandment and Deuteronomy 4:15–19. The first commandment forbids the worship of any false god, and the second demands that we do not worship the true God in an unworthy manner. It is not enough to worship the correct God. We must worship the correct God *correctly!*[2]

Moses reminds the people that when Jehovah spoke to them in the valley of Horeb, they heard a voice but "you saw no form." And so he warns them, "Watch yourselves very carefully, so that you do not become corrupt and make for yourselves an idol, an image of any shape" (Deuteronomy 4:15–16). In keeping with this, Calvin notes, "Whatever forms of God man devises are diametrically opposed to His nature; therefore, as soon as idols appear, true religion is corrupted and adulterated."

Paul urges his listeners in Athens not to think that the divine being is like gold or silver or stone—an image made by man's design and skill (Acts 17:29). Although the claim is often heard, "By means of the image or form or structure, I feel closer to God," God warns against such things because all who seek visible forms of God are, irrespective of how they may feel, departing from Him. God, who invited us to draw near to Him, would not forbid anything that helped us to make the connection. By forbidding the use of images, whether metal or mental, God restrains our waywardness. He frees us from the stupidity and emptiness of our speculation when we live in obedience to this command.

The straightforward nature of the second commandment comes across clearly in the Heidelberg Catechism:

> *Question 96: What is God's will for us in the second commandment?*
>
> Answer: That we in no way make any image of God, nor worship Him in any other way than He has commanded in His word.
>
> *Question 97: May we then not make any image at all?*
>
> Answer: God cannot and may not be visibly portrayed in any way, although creatures may be portrayed. Yet, God forbids making or having such images if one's intention is to worship them, or to serve God through them.
>
> *Question 98: But may not images be permitted in the churches as teaching aids for the unlearned?*
>
> Answer: No. We should not try to be wiser than God. He wants His people instructed by the living preaching of His word, not by idols that cannot ever talk.

In light of the clarity of this exposition, I am at pains to understand the actions of a church in Alabama. I have in my files an article from the religious section of a Birmingham newspaper and a large photograph of a man painting on a canvas in the pulpit. The journalist describes how, in the time normally allotted to the sermon, the pastor had invited this artist to paint a picture.

This may seem to some to be a trivial matter hardly worthy of mention, but it reveals the extent to which God's Word is being set aside. No matter how excellent the painting may have been, it cannot and must not be allowed to take the place of the proclamation of His Word. Calvin said, "Because God does not speak to us every day from the heavens, there are only the scriptures in which He has willed that His truth should be published." This commandment offers no loopholes. God is opposed to any representation of Himself. His people are not to make an idol "in the form of anything." "Don't look for me in shrines or paintings or statues," the Lord might say, "I'm not there. Look for me in my Word."

Calvin has a section in the *Institutes* where he argues that as long as doctrine was pure and strong the church rejected images. If we look around the contemporary scene, it will quickly become apparent that where there is an absence of gospel preaching there is a greater likelihood of finding superstitious rituals. I recall standing in a church building in Chicago and watching people kneeling before material representations of deity. I don't for a moment question their motivation, but it made me wonder whether they did not imagine that some power of divinity was present there. Again Calvin observes, "when you prostrate yourself in veneration, representing to yourself in an image either a god or a creature, you are already ensnared in some superstition. This is foolish in the extreme."

Isaiah asks, "To whom, then, will you compare God? What image will you compare him to?" (Isaiah 40:18). Since all things were created by God and are subject to Him, it makes no sense at all to think of fashioning anything that could ever represent the Creator of the universe. When we set aside this commandment by tolerating images in worship, our understanding of God is inevitably distorted. The individuals whom I observed kneeling in Chicago were bowed before a crucifix. Jesus on the cross speaks to us of His suffering, which it is clearly right for us to ponder. But a Jesus on a cross is limited to the pathos of all that scene represents. It conveys nothing of His power, victory, and glory. He is now having completed the work of redemption seated at the right hand of the Father on high. So a static image of Christ on the cross is a distortion of the total picture.

Imagination is a wonderful gift, but when we use it to conjure up our own image of God it leads us astray. It is quite common to hear people say, "I like to think of God as . . . " and then add whatever picture they have in mind. The problem is that our view of God is to be defined by His revelation of Himself in the Bible, and when we conceive of Him apart from that, it will be misleading at best. Anything we imagine will be inevitably less then God, and when that which is less than God is used to portray God, we are led quickly to blasphemy and idolatry.

Exodus 32 contains the record of the fashioning of the golden calf. "We don't know what's happened to Moses" they tell Aaron. "He's somewhere out there talking with God but we want to know that God is present with us so make us gods who may go before us." Instead of admonishing them for their impatience, unbelief, and disobedience, Aaron took their gold and fashioned it into a calf.

Upon completion he hears the people exclaiming, "These are your gods, O Israel, who brought you up out of Egypt" (v. 4).

Upon hearing that, we might have expected him to melt

the whole project down, realizing that he'd made a dreadful mistake. Instead, he compounds the problem by building an altar in front of the calf and announcing plans for a festival to the Lord. He was naïve at best. Did he think that this solid gold calf would remind the people that Yahweh was powerful? The golden calf did nothing to display God's glory and everything to distort it. The result was revelry and chaos. When we get the worship wrong, chaos ensues. Paul described the process in Romans 1:24. To exchange the truth of God for a lie: to exchange the glory of the immortal God for images made to look like mortal man and birds and animals and reptiles is to become susceptible to the sinful desires of the human heart issuing in adultery, homosexuality and every kind of wickedness.

In all of this, God is dishonored. In November 1993 two thousand women gathered in Minneapolis for what must have been the most bizarre and dreadful conference of the final decade of the twentieth century. From a position of radical feminism they sought to "re-imagine" a new god and a new road to salvation. They rejected the orthodox view of the incarnation and atonement of Jesus Christ as being nothing other than a patriarchal construct, which they blamed for the oppression of women. The attendees blessed, thanked, and praised Sophia as a deity who was with God at creation and whom they described as "the tree of life to those who lay hold of her." The crass foolishness of the whole event is aptly summarized in a quote from the Chinese feminist Kwok Pui-Lan: "If we cannot imagine Jesus as a tree, as a river, as wind, and as rain, we are doomed together."[3] The final phrase, "we are doomed together," is accurate, but not for the reason she suggests. Rather, it is for rejecting Him in whom all God's fullness dwells in bodily form. "We know . . .

that the Son of God has come and has given us understanding, so that we may know him who is true" (1 John 5:20).

If we are to escape the corruption that accompanies all attempts at worshipping God by means of likenesses, pictures, and imaginings, then we must focus on the Lord Jesus Himself, who is "the image of the invisible God" (Colossians 1:15).

To obey this command sets us free from vain imaginings, strange superstitions, and improper and inadequate views of God so that we might learn to worship Him in spirit and in truth. We will return to this positive side of the equation, but we must first pay attention to the warning that is added in Exodus 20:5–6, "For I, the LORD your God, am a jealous God, punishing the children for the sin of the fathers to the third and fourth generation of those who hate me, but showing love to a thousand generations of those who love me and keep my commandments." As in the first commandment, God's demand is based upon who He is. Here He tells us that He is a jealous God. In the same way that a husband is unprepared to share his wife's love and affection with anyone else, so God is jealous of His honor. He will not share His glory and demands that our worship of Him be utterly uncorrupted.

I recall some years ago being asked by a couple on the threshold of marriage whether there was a place for fantasy in their expressions of love towards each other. The man had apparently been influenced by someone who was suggesting that the marriage bed would be enhanced by entertaining thoughts of others while giving attention to his wife. We didn't have to talk about it for very long before they were convinced that the exclusivity of their loyalty must be expressed in a monogamy that was mental as well as physical. In Hosea, God describes His relationship with His people in terms of being betrothed to them in righteousness (Hosea

2:19–20). Like a jealous husband, He is unwilling to settle for the kind of worshippers who draw near with their lips (physically) but whose hearts are far from Him (mentally) (Isaiah 29:13; Matthew 15:8–9).

The "threatening" words in Exodus 20:5–6 concerning the punishing of the children for the sins of the fathers are a reminder to us that when we disobey the commands of God we do not do so in isolation. The consequences may run for generations. "Each generation stands in a place of mounting guilt, under the accumulating sins of the fathers."[4]

This is not the place to try and tackle this issue exhaustively. A few comments will help, I hope, to keep us on track and point us in the right direction.

We should read this text in conjunction with Ezekiel 18:20, where God declares that He will not punish the innocent for another's offense. We should not miss the fact that this is not a word of judgment to be pronounced upon the children but a word of warning provided for the parents. Fathers and mothers are here called to count the cost of the effect their sin will have upon their families. One generation turns its back on God, and the next grows up without Him. All sin has a "domino" effect, and parents ought to ponder the punishment their children will face for their own sins, which they have learned from the sorry example of their parents. Take, for example, the impact on a child who grows up in a home where the name of God is routinely blasphemed. We should consider the warning to those who hate Him in light of the promise to those whose love is expressed in obedience. "He commends to us the largeness of His mercy, which He extends to a thousand generations, while He has assigned only four generations to His vengeance."[5]

We know, too, that the children of the wicked sometimes reform and those of believers sometimes degenerate.

Although this warning doesn't always take effect, it is issued with sufficient force so as to comfort the righteous and to alarm the wicked.

Now, as promised, we turn to the "positive" side of this commandment. One of the rules for interpreting the Ten Commandments is that the negative commandments ("You shall not . . .") include positive commands, and vice versa. So if the second commandment forbids us to worship the true God in any unworthy manner, it simultaneously calls us to worship Him properly. No one who desires to please God would dispute this. But it is very obvious that there is significant disagreement among God's people over the content, structure, style, and emphasis of proper worship.

It is no exaggeration to say that we were created to praise. The psalmist writes, he says, for a future generation, "that a people not yet created may praise the LORD" (Psalm 102:18).

When Jesus talks to the woman at the well in Samaria He tells her that the Father is seeking true worshipers (John 4:21–24). Given that this is such a spiritual priority, it should be no surprise to us to discover that the Evil One seeks to make it an occasion of confusion and division among God's people. For at least the past decade, probably longer, I have discovered in traveling that in this area God's people have been outwitted by the devil's schemes. Having said that, it is also fairly obvious that churches without any outside assistance from our archenemy have managed to tolerate, and in some cases foster, chaos in this most vital area. I have long thought to address this at length and in print.

There is only space for a few observations. When we talk about worshiping God, we must first recognize that this involves far more than the corporate gathering of God's people on the Lord's Day. The Shorter Catechism starts us on the right track in its answer to the first question, "What is the chief end of man?" "Man's chief end is to glorify God and to enjoy Him forever." In my reading this morning, Spurgeon issued a reminder, which ties in with this. We are here that we may "live unto the Lord," he says. "We remain on earth as sowers to scatter good seed; as ploughmen to break up the fallow ground; as herald's publishing salvation. We are here as the 'salt of the earth', to be a blessing to the world. We are here to glorify Christ in our daily life. . . . Let us live earnest, useful, holy lives, to 'the praise of the glory of His grace.'"[6]

We worship God in response to His mercy as we offer our bodies as living sacrifices. The hymn writer captured this in the line, "Take my moments and my days, let them flow in ceaseless praise." With minds renewed, in our time, talents, tasks, relationships, and hobbies, whatever we do, we "do it all to the glory of God" (1 Corinthians 10:31). Perhaps part of our problem in thinking about worship stems from our not having a big enough picture. Instead of viewing worship as a lifestyle, we are tempted to think of it as an event, something that takes place in certain buildings at prescribed times. When God's people learn to worship through the week, then what happens on the Lord's Day is the corporate overflow of lives in touch with God. So when the call to worship is given, it does not call them to unfamiliar activity but to the corporate expression of what has been their individual and family focus. When the Word of God is read and the preacher worships in declaring God's mighty acts, then the believer's soul is stirred and he is thankful for those who had encouraged him saying, "Let us go to the house of the Lord."

Since the second commandment forbids the use of images as we worship God, and the New Testament reveals that God has provided the only true and worthy image of Himself in the Lord Jesus, who is "the image of the invisible God" (Colossians 1:15); then our worship as we gather is to be framed by biblical principles. Christian worship is unlike any other event. Our objective is not to make outsiders comfortable but to worship God in such a fashion that they may say, "Surely God is in this place."

There are many occasions when in reaching out to unbelievers we will seek to ensure that we are removing for them all unnecessary hurdles in hearing the message. But this is not to be our focus when we gather in worship. The unbeliever should find himself stirred to ask, *Why do those people sing with such enthusiasm? Why do they listen with such care? Why do they speak to God with such devotion? What is it about me that I have no such appetite for God or His Word?* Such a perspective, I know, flies in the face of what would appear to be the prevailing mood in large segments of evangelicalism. But the challenge must be presented to what is an increasingly man-centered, me-oriented approach to worship. Our images are of the cheerleader and the stand up comedian, of the jazz quartet in the corner of the restaurant, and it is all so horizontal. We are unlikely in those settings to be confronted with the transcendent majesty of God before whom we will one day stand in judgment and who desires to meet with us as we gaze upon His glory in the face of Jesus.

The style of worship, however, will vary from culture to culture and from family to family. This should be no surprise. Whether I find myself in the western isles of Scotland singing metrical psalms without any musical accompaniment, or in the prayer-book service of an Anglican church, or in Kenya with the rhythmic drumming of African culture, or in the orchestrated praise of the Midwest of America, I am committed to making the most of every opportunity for worship. My own personal preferences regarding style need to take a very definite second place to the call to worship in spirit and in truth.

Here at Parkside we have chosen to be guided in our choice of hymnody and song by two questions. First, are the words true to Scripture and do they focus my mind on who God is and what He has done? And second, is the tune such as can be sung by the congregation without its form distracting from the content of the lyric. We are not "hung up" on the contemporary issue. Good lyrics and good tunes are not locked in any era. We have also never given consideration to having services that are distinguished by styles of worship. Whenever I see a church bulletin that lists "9 A.M. Traditional Service, and 11 A.M. Contemporary Service," I can't help feeling that there has been a failure on the part of leadership. The family unity must never be in anything or anyone else than the Lord Jesus. So instead of splitting up on the basis of worship style, we should learn to prefer one another as we discover the pattern that fits us all. We have been helped by constantly referring to certain fixed points. First, our worship is to be Trinitarian as we come to God the Father, through God the Son, and in God the Spirit. Then, as we have said, our worship is to be Christ-centered. It is to be biblical in that it is grounded in all that the Scriptures teach concerning the praise of God.

It is also to be rational. Our minds are to be stirred with truth rather than our feet being animated by rhythm. The latter may accompany the former but must never exist without it. The kind of mindlessness that evokes a form of repetitive praise is something we seek to avoid. Our worship does have an emotional dimension inasmuch as we recognize that worship is empty when the feelings of our hearts do not correspond with the expression of our lips.

Most of all, we acknowledge that worship is a spiritual exercise. We must be spiritually alive. Dead men don't sing. We need to be spiritually assisted. Filled with God's Spirit we then sing and make music in our heart to the Lord. We must then be spiritually active. We are not listening to the choir. We are the choir. We are not spectators. We are participants. We come asking God to help us to set aside every idolatrous thought so that we might be the kind of worshippers the Father seeks.

It would be wonderful if what was said about the Thessalonians could be said of us: "They tell how you turned to God from idols to serve the living and true God."

3

WHAT'S
IN A NAME?

You shall not misuse the name of the LORD your
God, for the LORD will not hold anyone guiltless
who misuses his name.

—EXODUS 20:7

*O*n January 8, the year of our Lord 1697, at two o'clock in
the afternoon, Thomas Aikenhead was taken to the gallows
on the road between Edinburgh and Leith. The hangman
pulled away the ladder, the body swung, and the theology
student, not quite nineteen, was dead. His crime? Blasphemy!

An act of the Scottish parliament in 1695 decreed that a
person "not distracted in his wits" who railed or cursed
against God or persons of the Trinity was to be punished
with death. In prosecuting the case, James Stewart, the Lord
Advocate (the Scottish equivalent of Attorney General), addressed the accused: "It is of verity, that you Thomas Aikenhead shaking off all fear of God and regard to his majestic
laws, have now for more than a twelvemonth made it as it
were your endeavor and work to vent your wicked blas-
phemies against God and our Savior Jesus Christ."

My purpose in beginning here is clearly not to argue for

the reenactment of the blasphemy laws of seventeenth century Scotland. It is rather to provide a dramatic backdrop against which to consider the way in which our culture endorses blasphemy as a way of life. The name of God is routinely misused by all ages and in all places. This is not new. The psalmist addressed the same issue in his generation. His words have a contemporary ring.

> Remember how the enemy has mocked you, O LORD,
>   how foolish people have reviled your name.
>   —PSALM 74:18

In considering each of the commandments, it is important for us to keep in mind certain principles of interpretation. (a) The commandments are spiritual and therefore require that we obey them from our hearts. Outward conformity must be the product of inward affection. (b) There is a positive and negative aspect to each commandment. Where a sin is forbidden, a duty is commanded; where a duty is commanded, a sin is implied. (c) Each commandment forbids not only the acts of sin but also the desire and inclination to sin. So where a sin is forbidden, what leads to that sin is also forbidden.[1]

So we see that the third commandment on the negative side forbids every wrong use of God's name and on the positive side demands that we use His name with reverence and awe. Why is this so important? The straightforward answer: because God's name is more than just a title. His name declares His character. It proclaims who He is and what He does. The name of God comes to stand realistically for God Himself. So, for example, Solomon writes, "The name of the LORD is a strong tower; the righteous run to it and are safe" (Proverbs 18:10).

By naming Himself in a variety of ways, God graciously accommodates Himself to our finite thinking. "Is it not an inestimable goodness that our God so stoops toward us and permits us to use his name?"[2] "Only God truly knows God."[3] "Our creaturehood requires God to reveal himself if we are to have adequate knowledge of him." We find ourselves echoing the saying of Agur:

I have not learned wisdom,
    nor have I the knowledge of the Holy One.
Who has gone up to heaven and come down?
    Who has gathered up the wind in the hollow of his hands?
Who has wrapped up the waters in his cloak?
    Who has established all the ends of the earth?
What is his name, and the name of his son?
    Tell me if you know!
                        —PROVERBS 30:3–4

Bruce Milne says:

There is no road from man's intellectual and moral perception to a genuine knowledge of God. The only way to knowledge of God is for God freely to place himself within the range of our perception, and renew our fallen understanding. Hence, if we are to know God and have any adequate basis for our Christian understanding and experience, revelation is indispensable.[4]

In this third commandment we discover that God jealously guards His name. He expects His friends to do likewise. Our Asian and African friends are much more familiar with this concept than we are in the West. When we attend a conference, we are given a nametag. How apt. We wear these, not because they say something about our character but simply to enable us to distinguish Bill from Tom and Mary from Jane. Derek Prime writes of an American living among the Masai in Tanzania who bandied names about with great ease. He had to learn that the Masai regarded this as very rude because in public and with strangers they did not use personal names. They chose instead to use titles or designations. One day a Masai man said to him: "Do not throw my name about. My name is important. My name is me. My name is for my friends."[5] When someone is dear to us, we do not like to think of anyone making fun of his name. It is offensive when people gossip about him or otherwise misuse his name. Surely it is inconceivable that what we would demand for a friend we would deny to our Lord and God!

This is in accord with the first petition of the Lord's Prayer, "Hallowed be Thy name." To hallow the majesty of His name means, says Calvin, "That we are not to profane His name by treating it contemptuously and irreverently. . . . We should be zealous and careful to honor His name with godly reverence" (*Institutes* 2.8.22). As a church we have sought to remind ourselves of this by chiseling in granite at the entrance of our building the words of Psalm 138:2, "You have exalted above all things your name and your word."

As we study His Word, we learn His name and all that it means. The Bible makes clear that the name of God is precious and unique. Contemporary society has little or no concept of this at all. As someone has put it: "Now in the twenty-first century the letters *g-o-d* spell nothing." Obedience to the third commandment will serve to distinguish those who know and love God from those who do not. Sadly, it is not uncommon to hear the same disregard for God's name coming from the lips of professing Christians. Commenting on this in his day, Calvin said, "Although many pretend to be Christians, nevertheless they have never been known to be such, nor to worship God, nor pay him homage, nor render him that service which is properly his. For how does the name of God fare?"

Such laxity towards the sanctity of God's name, both then and now, is further evidence of the need to reaffirm the abiding place of the Law in the life of the Christian as a rule of life, lived in love to the Lord Jesus. Here is an obvious application of what it means to present our bodies as living sacrifices. Instead of allowing the contemporary culture to squeeze us into its mold, we will join the psalmist in declaring by word and life: "O LORD, our Lord, how majestic is your name in all the earth!" (Psalm 8:1). As our minds are renewed by the sanctifying power of God's Word, we not only learn what the name of God means but also why it matters.

In Exodus 3 we have the record of Moses encounter with God, which took place in the context of a familiar sight, a burning bush, with an unfamiliar dimension: though the bush was on fire, it did not burn up. Having got the attention of Moses, God then spoke to him from within the bush. When Moses grasped God's plan for him to go to Pharaoh and request the release of the Israelite captives, Moses asked:

> "Suppose I go to the Israelites and say to them, 'The God of your fathers has sent me to you,' and they ask me, 'What is his name?' Then what shall I tell them?" God said to Moses, "I AM WHO I AM. This is what you are to say to the Israelites: 'I AM has sent me to you.'"
>
> —EXODUS 3:13–14

We may find this to be a little bewildering until we remind ourselves that the name of God stands realistically for

God Himself. The "name" of God declares what God is (His essence) and what He does (His works). By means of this name, God declares Himself to be, "self-existing, self-determining, and sovereign."[6] The prophet Jeremiah compares the worthless idols of the nations with the power and majesty of the Lord Almighty who is the maker of all things.

God declares Himself to be "self-existing, self-determining, and sovereign," says Calvin, "that we are not to profane His name by treating it contemptuously and irreverently. . . . We should be zealous and careful to honor His name with godly reverence" (*Institutes* 2.8.22).

> Like a scarecrow in a melon patch,
>> their idols cannot speak;
>> they must be carried because they cannot walk.
> Do not fear them;
>> they can do no harm nor can they do any good.
>> —JEREMIAH 10:5

These "gods" of human contrivance are worthless, the objects of mockery. In direct contrast, listen to how the prophet addresses the true and living God.

> No one is like you, O LORD;
>> you are great,
>> and your name is mighty in power.
> Who should not revere you,
>> O King of the nations?
>> This is your due.
> Among all the wise men of the nations
>> and in all their kingdoms,
>> there is no one like you.
>> —JEREMIAH 10:6–7

IN HIS WORLD

It is not unusual for my wife to identify the manufacturer of a piece of furniture by simply observing its style and structure. When I am tempted to doubt her, she has me open one of the drawers, and there in its usual place is the stamp of the maker. When we look at the created world, we find that each part of it is stamped with the Maker's signature. "Since the creation of the world God's invisible qualities —his eternal power and divine nature—have been clearly seen, being understood from what has been made, so that men are without excuse" (Romans 1:20). The psalmist reminds us that the voice of creation declares the mighty power of God's name. The voice of creation transcends all barriers of human language. The voice of creation "goes out into all the earth, their words to the ends of the world" (see Psalm 19:1–4). The text of Isaac Watts' hymn "I Sing the Mighty Power of God" contains this verse.

> *There's not a plant or flower below,*
>
> *But makes Thy glories known;*
>
> *And clouds arise, and tempests blow,*
>
> *By order from Thy throne;*
>
> *While all that borrows life from Thee*
>
> *Is ever in Thy care,*
>
> *And everywhere that man can be,*
>
> *Thou, God, art present there.*

In His Son

God's name is declared in His Word. It is majestic, trust-worthy, powerful, and good, and it endures forever. "When we turn to the Holy Scripture we find there an image by means of which God more particularly reveals himself to us than he does in the sky or on the earth. Neither the sun nor the moon, albeit they give clarity to the world—reveal the majesty of God as much as the law, the prophets and the gospel."[7]

God's name is declared not only in the written word, but uniquely and supremely in the Lord Jesus, who is the Living Word. We have a record of Jesus' prayer prior to his arrest and crucifixion. "I have manifested Your name to the men whom You gave Me out of the world" (John 17:6 NASB; "re-vealed you," NIV). Jesus is declaring that by His words and His life and His character the fullness of the Godhead has lived in bodily form. When Philip, one of the disciples, asked Jesus to show them the Father, Jesus replied: "Anyone who has seen me has seen the Father" (John 14:9). It is es-pecially important at this point in history when there is such confused thinking about the nature of God that the Christian is convinced and convincing in this matter. In teaching our children basic Bible truths we ask them: "How many Gods are there?" They reply, "There is only one God." "I am the LORD, and there is no other; apart from me there is no God" (Isaiah 45:5). We then inquire concerning the number and identity of the persons in the one God. On the strength of Matthew 28:19 they respond, "There are three persons. The Father, the Son, and the Holy Spirit."

As parents we must pay careful attention to the words of Moses:

Hear, O Israel: The LORD our God, the LORD is one. Love
the LORD your God with all your heart and with all your
soul and with all your strength. These commandments that
I give you today are to be upon your hearts. Impress them
on your children. Talk about them when you sit at home
and when you walk along the road, when you lie down and
when you get up.

—DEUTERONOMY 6:4–7

It is not difficult to find evidence that points to the neglect of this parental duty. Surely one of the most alarming
signs of our culture's slide towards Gomorrah is in the blas-
phemous language on the lips of even small children. One
generation turns its back on God and the next generation
grows up with little to no knowledge of Him at all. Norman
Rockwell's painting of the family bowing their heads to give
thanks for their meal is a museum piece. It serves as a reminder of the days when God was clearly regarded as the
source, sustainer, and end of all things. Since then, man's
view of God has declined. God is a name for whatever man
thinks or feels Him to be. God is viewed as limited and
proves upon inspection to be created in man's image. Such a
deity is always kind, helpful, loving, and never judgmental!
The ideal personal God is devoid of any moral dimension at
all. He turns a blind eye to all our failings and tolerates our
strange beliefs and our bad behavior. This view of God is
popular in many quarters.

It is matched by the idea of God as a cosmic principle.
An energizing principle, if you like—the force that goes with
you, a modern Jedi knight. When man conceives of God in
either of these ways, it is not surprising that he has no concern whatsoever about the misuse of God's name. After all, a
scarecrow in a melon patch has to be carried, propped up,

and clearly has no feelings (Jeremiah 10:5). When Paul encountered the idols in Athens and the religious confusion they represented, he began where we need to begin today. He told them that the living and true God is not the product of man's imagination. He is the "Lord of heaven and earth and does not live in temples built by hands" (Acts 17:24). He made the earth by His power, and it was by His wisdom that the world was established and He stretched out the heavens by His understanding (see Job 38). I can still recall a sermon by J. I. Packer in which he provided the following summary. Addressing the phrase "The LORD he is God" (Deuteronomy 4:35, 39; Psalm 100:3 all KJV), he made four statements concerning the nature and character of God.

1. He Is Plural.

He is tri-personal—three persons in an abiding, eternal fellowship of love and togetherness: the Father, the Son, and the Holy Spirit. There are not three Gods but one God in three persons. This three-ness is a Christian revelation. The one and only Lord, the Creator, guide, and goal of history is not imagined by man, but discloses Himself. The word we use to describe this is *Trinity*. The concept is biblical, although the word itself is not found in Scripture. In the doctrine of the Trinity we have a formulation rather than an explanation of this mind-stretching truth.

2. He Is Powerful.

The first statement answered the question, "Who is God?" This statement tells us how He exists. All created things run down, but not the Creator. He derives life and energy from Himself. He is eternal, uncreated, infinite, and not limited by time or space or any dimension of the world He has made, or by any power or agency within that world. God is, as we have noted, self-existent. In contrast, our existence is due wholly to His gracious power and providence. The glory of man is like the flower of the field, which quickly wilts and withers. The glory of God is like the burning bush, which burned and was not consumed and which provides us with a picture of the endless energy of God.

3. He Is Perfect.

In Exodus we have the description of the goodness of the Lord passing before Moses as the Lord proclaimed His name in His servant's presence.

> And he passed in front of Moses, proclaiming, "The LORD, the LORD, the compassionate and gracious God, slow to anger, abounding in love and faithfulness, maintaining love to thousands, and forgiving wickedness, rebellion and sin. Yet he does not leave the guilty unpunished."
> —EXODUS 34:6–7

If we ask, "How does God act?" The answer is, "Absolutely perfectly." He is infinite in His goodness. How can God punish sin and yet grant forgiveness to the sinner? The hymn writer has the answer.

> O safe and happy shelter!
>
> O refuge tried and sweet!
>
> O trysting-place where heaven's love
>
> And heaven's justice meet!

He refers of course to the cross of the Lord Jesus, for it is there that God's love and justice meet. In the judgment, this perfect God's verdict will be absolutely fair and absolutely final.

4. He Is Praiseworthy.

Here we find ourselves face-to-face with the positive side of the third commandment. It requires that we use the holy name of God only with reverence and awe, so that we may properly confess Him, pray to Him, and praise Him in everything we do and say. The Shorter Scottish Catechism concurs with the previous sentence from the Heidelberg when it begins with the declaration: "The chief end of man is to glorify God and to enjoy him forever." Glory is what God shows us of Himself and it is what we are to give Him in response. It is only in such praise that we discover our true humanness. Man is standing on his head in asking the question, "Who or what does God think He is, commanding me to revere His name?" He needs to be turned the right way up and then he will learn to ask in humble wonder. "What is man that you are mindful of him?" (Psalm 8:4).

We live in a society that has little place if any for God. He is regarded as a personal notion or a cosmic principle. If that has been your perspective, then it is time to confess your ignorance or your willful defiance and to cast yourself upon His mercy. And Timothy tells us, "Everyone who confesses the name of the Lord must turn away from wickedness" (2 Timothy 2:19). According to this commandment, we must learn to avoid the ways in which God's name is used wrongly and we must devote ourselves to honor and reverence His name. We will be helped by following the pattern of the Shorter Catechism, which considers the commandment first from the positive side and then from the negative.

What Is Required
in the Third Commandment?

We are required to use "God's names, titles, attributes, ordinances, word, and works" in a holy and reverent manner (response to Question 54, the Shorter Catechism). How will this be worked out in practical terms? The Larger Catechism specifically refers to "thought, meditation, word and writing; by a holy profession, and answerable conversation" (response to Question 112). Thinking in terms of the following four words has helped me.

Thinking

Becoming a Christian is a mind-altering experience. Paul refers to this in his second letter to Corinth. Before we were reconciled to God we thought about Jesus and ourselves and others in a certain way. Our minds, says Calvin, were crammed with falsehood and wicked imaginations conceived against the honor of God. But now, in Christ, our perspective has been radically altered. Peter explained to his readers that he had written both of his letters to them "as reminders to stimulate you to wholesome thinking" (2 Peter 3:1). The way in which we think about God in the privacy of our own thoughts is really the measure of our commitment to this third commandment. Since these commandments are spiritual, they go to the heart and require from us an obedience that is internal. God is not interested in our ability to maintain an external, legal observance of His Law by means of self-effort. He perceives our thoughts from afar and His Word judges the thoughts and attitudes of our heart. He spoke to His people through the prophet Jeremiah: "O Jerusalem, wash the evil from your heart and be saved. How long will you harbor wicked thoughts?" (Jeremiah 4:14). We will do well in the keeping of this commandment by following the example of the psalmist, who meditated on God's works and gave serious consideration to all that God had accomplished.

Praying

I recently sat around the dining table with a family I did not know well. I quickly learned a great deal about the teenagers' relationship with their father. I simply listened to the way in which they addressed him. By their words and their demeanor they revealed at least something of the attitude of their hearts.

The same is true in our relationship with our heavenly Father. The way in which we approach Him says a great deal about our desire to hallow and revere His name. There is a huge difference between the interest of a religious man in learning the appropriate terminology to be able to *say* prayers and the earnest heartfelt cry of the child, "Daddy, Daddy help me" (see Romans 8:15). Such intimacy is not irreverent. It honors God because in calling out for His help we do so on the basis of all that His name means.

- He is the Lord who provides—*Jehovah-Jireh* (Genesis 22:14).
- He is my peace—*Jehovah-Shalom* (Judges 6:24).
- "The LORD is my shepherd"—*Jehovah-Rohi* (Psalm 23:1).
- He is our righteousness—*Jehovah-Zidkenu* (Jeremiah 23:6).

One of the ways in which the followers of Jesus are described in Acts is as "those who call on this name" (Acts 9:21). Paul urges his young understudy, Timothy, to pursue righteous living in the company of those who "call on the Lord out of a pure heart" (2 Timothy 2:22).

Speaking

We keep the third commandment not only in the way we speak to God but also in the way in which we speak about Him. The Puritan Philip Brooks said, "We know metals by their tinkling and men by their talking." Solomon tells us that "the tongue has the power of life and death" (Proverbs 18:21). We may speak of God in a way that is helpful. We do so when we speak of Him in a way that is honest and careful and in keeping with all that He has made known of Himself in His Word and in His Son. The Christian will not speak of weather being brought to us by Mother Nature but instead of the majesty of the Creator God displayed in sunshine and in storm.

> In his hand are the depths of the earth,
>   and the mountain peaks belong to him.
> The sea is his, for he made it,
>   and his hands formed the dry land.
> —PSALM 95:4–5

It is also possible to speak about God in a manner that is harmful as, for example, when Jacob employed God's name in the deception of his father, Isaac: "The LORD your God gave me success" (Genesis 27:20). He was taking God's name in vain. We must not follow his bad example.

Walking

We reveal our commitment to the positive side of this commandment not only in our talking but also in our walking. The prophet Micah distinguishes between the surrounding nations and the people of God when he declares, "All the nations may walk in the name of their gods; we will walk in the name of the LORD our God for ever and ever" (Micah 4:5). This is in accord with the opening of the psalms, where the Lord's servant is not to be found walking in the counsel of the wicked. Instead he is delighting in the Law of the Lord that provides us with a comprehensive statement of God's nature, which is embodied in His name (Psalm 1). The man who honors God's name is the man who walks in humility before Him. "He has showed you, O man, what is good. And what does the LORD require of you? To act justly and to love mercy and to walk humbly with your God" (Micah 6:8).

WHAT IS FORBIDDEN
IN THE THIRD COMMANDMENT?

The third commandment forbids the profaning and abusing of God's name. There are clearly many ways in which it is possible to violate this command by misusing God's name; for our purposes we will select just four.

Perjury

The most basic prohibition in this third commandment concerns taking God's name and attaching it to a statement that is false. "Do not swear falsely by my name and so profane the name of your God. I am the LORD" (Leviticus 19:12).

"When a man makes a vow to the LORD . . . [he] must do everything he said" (Numbers 30:2). When we make vows and break them, we take God's name in vain. God is always true to Himself. He always keeps His word. For us to employ His name in the interests of falsehood is to misuse His name.

We need to pay careful attention to this. It seems that most people think of the real issue addressed in this command as being profanity (a profane use of the divine name) rather than a dishonest pledging of one's word (perjury). (For a good and concise treatment of the wider implications of this subject, see John Stott, *The Message of the Sermon on the Mount*.[8]) Some teach in light of Jesus' words concerning oaths that as Christians we are categorically forbidden from taking any kind of oath, even when required in a court of law. Stott says, however, "What Jesus emphasized in his teaching was that honest men do not need to resort to oaths; it was not that they should refuse to take an oath if required by some external authority to do so."[9]

Blasphemy

We are guilty of blasphemy when we take God's name, which is sacred, and treat it with irreverence or contempt. The extent to which we tolerate this in evangelical circles is shameful. Whether it is in referring to the God and Father of our Lord Jesus Christ as "the man upstairs" or in carelessly mouthing expressions such as "Good Lord," "Lord have mercy," and even "Oh, my God," we are guilty of profaning God's name. What kind of company is prepared to produce T-shirts with slogans like "This blood's for you." It is difficult to imagine such a product selling well in seventeenth-century Scotland! We might expect such profanity from a

godless culture but not from within the marketing depart-
ments of Christian merchandising. We do not take seriously
enough the warning passages in Hebrews.

> Anyone who rejected the law of Moses died without mercy
> on the testimony of two or three witnesses. How much
> more severely do you think a man deserves to be punished
> who has trampled the Son of God under foot, who has
> treated as an unholy thing the blood of the covenant that
> sanctified him, and who has insulted the Spirit of grace?
> —HEBREWS 10:28–29

Flippancy

Flippancy is a cousin of profanity. It is often a compan-
ion to fluency. Proverbs reminds us that when words are
many, sin is not absent. The old chestnut hits the mark: "An
unbridled tongue is the chariot of the devil." We are guilty
of this when we sprinkle God's name in our conversation in
a manner that is superficial or insincere. It is clearly possible
for us to say right things in wrong ways. Too often in Christian circles we say things just to be heard saying them.

I recall as a teenager reading a book on prayer by Rosa-
lind Rinker. In it she told of how as a new Christian she was
moved to tears in the prayer meetings. There was a gravity
about this divine engagement that stirred her spirit. She then
went on to tell of how after some time had elapsed and she
had become proficient in the phraseology and clichés of
prayer, she found it all too easy to engage in vain repetitions.

Many of us, if we are honest, can identify with her experience. We may have begun to treat serious matters lightly,
and our superficiality has paved the way for disrespect. We
need to repent of such an attitude and pay attention to

Calvin's exhortation to be so disposed in mind and speech that we neither think or say anything concerning God and His mysteries without reverence and much soberness. God had strong words for the false prophets who stole from each other words, which supposedly were from God. "I am against the prophets who wag their own tongues and yet declare, 'The LORD declares'" (Jeremiah 23:31). They were guilty of playing fast and loose with truth, and the result was that they led God's people astray with their reckless lies.

Hypocrisy

We violate the third commandment when our worship of God is marked by unreality.

> "These people come near to me with their mouth
>   and honor me with their lips,
>   but their hearts are far from me.
> Their worship of me
>   is made up only of rules taught by men."
>   —ISAIAH 29:13

When the Pharisees used God's name in evading their responsibility to their parents, Jesus confronted their hypocrisy in no uncertain terms. "You hypocrites! Isaiah was right when he prophesied about you" (Matthew 15:7). They had come up with a clever scam that allowed a man to divert money to himself (which he should have used to support his parents) by declaring it Corban, "a gift offered to God." Although the specifics may be different today, we dare not assume ourselves to be above such subterfuge. The sin of hypocrisy is crouching at our door. It desires to have us in its grasp. We must, in God's strength, master it.

In working my way through this material I have had one name in mind. He penned what must surely be one of the greatest hymns ever written on the theme of the name of Christ.

How sweet the name of Jesus sounds

In a believer's ear!

It soothes his sorrows, heals his wounds,

And drives away his fear.

What makes the lyric so remarkable is that it was written by one who had been notorious for his blasphemy. This captain of a slave trading ship in the eighteenth century was reported to have been masterful at inventing profanity. What a change in the life of John Newton, the author of "Amazing Grace." The Law of God confronted him with his sin and sent him to Christ for pardon. Having been placed in Christ, Newton then found the Law to be a means of grace, a minister of life as he set his feet upon its path. When he as a believer now read the third commandment, it did not condemn him, for Christ had silenced its condemnation by paying the wage it demanded. Newton must have discovered, as Alec Motyer puts it, that "The prohibitory 'You shall not . . .' had become the promissory 'You *shall* not . . .'"[10]

May we learn the same lesson and rejoice in being placed upon the pathway to freedom.

4

HOLY DAY
OR HOLIDAY?

Remember the Sabbath day by keeping it holy.

—EXODUS 20:8

𝒯he polling data tell us that Americans are a religious people, the large majority of whom attend church, believe in God, and pray daily. But you wouldn't know it from a typical Sunday, where the malls are hopping, the movie theaters packed, and the roads clogged with cars and bikers. Though we might still possibly remember the Sabbath day, in the land of perpetual fun we surely don't keep it holy.[1]

The story of the American Sunday described by Alexis McCrossen is one of declension. "Americans went from viewing Sunday as a holy day of rest, to a day of cultural enlightenment, to one of mindless consumption and amusements; they went from thinking of the day in terms of broad public purposes to goofing off or finding the best bargain."

The extent to which our view of Sunday has changed is aptly illustrated in this incident from the beginning of the nineteenth century.

In 1808 Hugh Wylie was removed from membership in his local Presbyterian Church in Western Pennsylvania. His offence? Opening the post office on Sunday and thus violating the fourth commandment. When the postmaster general ordered Wylie to continue distributing the mail whenever it arrived (including on Sunday) and the Presbyterian General Assembly upheld his exclusion, Wylie was forced to choose between his church and his job.[2] Those of us who find such circumstances hard to imagine will probably be intrigued to learn that it wasn't until 1949 that the National Football League officially sanctioned Sunday games. Fifty some years ago those who cared about the secularization of the country could surely not have envisioned Super Bowl Sunday in the American church. Buildings that are routinely dark on Sunday evenings (the Lord's Day having been completed by twelve noon) are opened especially for the Super Bowl and are ablaze with the color dancing on the large screens which bear the images of the gods of contemporary culture.

The fourth commandment more than any other forces us to wrestle with what we really believe about the abiding place of the Law in Christian living. Donald MacDonald, the minister of Greyfriars Free Church, Inverness, Scotland, began an address on the importance of the Lord's Day as follows:

> *We cannot help thinking that there are many things characterizing our day that make it very much more difficult for a true Christian to "walk with God" now than it used to be. It is the nature of every believer to seek communion with God, and, if he is in a healthy spiritual condition, he will use every available means to this end. We firmly believe that no other means is of more importance, or calculated to confer such great blessing on man as the Lord's Day.*

At the other end of the spectrum are those who argue that unlike the other nine, this command is optional.

By having church services on Saturday night, people can have the whole day on Sunday to go hiking, sailing, shopping, without being inconvenienced by having to attend services. We can just fit God into our schedules the way we do piano lessons and dental appointments. Then, if something more interesting comes along, we can always reschedule. McSabbath is here— worship services that are quick, easy, convenient, and user-friendly. Little or no sacrifice required.[3]

More alarming than any arguments that may ensue is the fact that for the majority it appears the issue is not debated, it is simply ignored. That the fourth commandment should engender strife is news to many who have never given any serious thought to the matter. They live with the assumption that such matters have to do with *then* and this is *now*. They have never considered the Lord's Day as a different day, one that is delightful by design and which helps to shape and frame our lives. That positive perspective has too often been obscured by the joyless mechanical externalism championed by the Pharisees and fashioned into an art form at times in Scotland!

The negative Sabbath of modern times seems to have originated in the bitter religious strife of the 17th century. In Scotland at that time, one poor wretch was hauled into court for smiling on the Sabbath; considering the state of Scotland in his day, he should have been congratulated for managing to smile at all!

Because some have hedged the Lord's Day with the thorns and thistles of human rules and regulations we must not react by dispensing with "the Day" but instead by clearing the weeds so as to reveal the beauty and benefit to body and soul. Already some readers are turning pages looking for the list of dos and don'ts. But this is to put the cart before the horse. We must first understand the principles before attempting the application.

We are to be transformed by the renewing of our minds —minds that are ruled by the Scriptures and free from every human directive that is additional to them. Until our consciences are bound by Scripture so that our actions are the product of conviction, we will be the victims of fluctuating fancies and susceptible to the "security" that is offered in conformity to a long list of human taboos. Convinced, grace-filled, spirit-led obedience to God's Law really is the pathway to freedom. Remember, the law is not the dynamic of our sanctification, God's love for us is not on the basis of duty, but neither does His love for us free us from duty. Our great need then with respect to the fourth command, in light of the swirling winds of confusion and uncertainty, is to recognize its perpetual obligation as part of the Moral Law.

> *God does not change; his moral perfections do not change; his moral law does not change. Times change; conditions change; we change. But under and through all there remains man's conscience, man's responsibility; and over all there is the unchanging holiness, justice and authority of God, issuing in the commands that bind man's conscience and, with a divine imperative must regulate his life, in one word, the moral law.*[4]

Our freedom from the law as a way of salvation does not mean that we are then free from the law as a guide to conduct. The fourth command is as much a part of that coherent "family code" as is any of the other nine. It is clear from even a cursory glance over the last century that in both church and society there was a shared sense of obligation to curtail both work and recreation on Sunday. What has changed? Are we to believe that for centuries our forefathers simply "got it wrong"? Did they fail to grasp the transition between Old and New Testament? Were they unable to grasp what Jesus meant when he declared that "the Sabbath was made for man"? Or is it possible that this commandment confronts us in a peculiar way with our unwillingness to "call it our supreme delight, to hear his dictates and obey."[5]

"Rebellious people do not want to rest in God's work or celebrate his creation. Like our first parents, we each want to be our own god. We want to rest in our own works and celebrate our own accomplishments."[6]

GOD RESTED AND SO MUST WE

"By the seventh day God had finished the work he had been doing; so on the seventh day he rested from all his work. And God blessed the seventh day and made it holy, because on it he rested from all the work of creating that he had done" Genesis 2:2–3).

The fourth commandment begins with a call to remember, to reflect upon the example of God Himself. In ceasing from His work he established the Sabbath—a day of rest after six days of work. He established the pattern after the grand scheme of His work of Creation. Clearly, He did not need to rest. Rather, He ceased from the work of creating while never ceasing from the work of sustaining and governing the world by His providential care. It is important for us to understand that the Sabbath was not instituted by men or even by Moses. It was not something unique for Israel. It was made from the very beginning for man.

"Then he said to them, 'The Sabbath was made for man, not man for the Sabbath. So the Son of Man is Lord even of the Sabbath'" (Mark 2:27–28). The context in which Jesus spoke these words is the occasion when the Pharisees accused His disciples of breaking the Sabbath by picking ears of corn. The law was clear on this matter: "If you enter your neighbor's grainfield, you may pick kernels with your hands, but you must not put a sickle to his standing grain" (Deuteronomy 23:25). But the Pharisees had added to God's law a whole catalogue of man-made, foolish regulations. They had distorted and perverted God's clear directive.

It is not uncommon to hear individuals quote Jesus' statement in Mark 2:27–8 in support of the notion that Jesus was setting aside the demands of the fourth commandment. The opposite is true. He was not canceling the use of the Sabbath, He was correcting the abuse of the Sabbath. "It was not deviation from Old Testament requirements that our Lord was condoning, but deviation from pharisaical distortion. He was condemning the tyranny by which the Sabbath institution had been made an instrument of oppression. And he did this by appeal to the true intent of the Sabbath as verified by Scripture itself."[7]

THE SCAFFOLDING IS NOT THE BUILDING

When the Ten Commandments are repeated in Deuteronomy 5, the wording differs slightly but obviously purposefully. Instead of *remember* the verb is *observe*. Here we discover the Sabbath being set within a framework that is distinctly Jewish. The people are to remember their deliverance from Egypt, and their Sabbath celebrations are signs of their unique relationship with God, and of their distinct identity, separating them from the surrounding nations. What God had given to all of mankind as a gift of creation we now find interwoven with the religious life of Israel. Here we find regulations that prohibit not only buying and selling but also the gathering of food and fuel and the lighting of fires in one's home on the Sabbath (Exodus 35:3).

Now it is here, if we are not careful, that we will find ourselves throwing the baby out with the proverbial bathwater. We dare not discard the Sabbath with the paraphernalia of Judaism. Under the Mosaic Law, working on the Sabbath was punishable by death (Exodus 35:2). Given the fact that this punishment is not applicable under the New Testament, are we then to conclude that the commandment itself is obsolete? No. By the same reasoning we would then set aside the fifth commandment and the seventh. Cursing one's parents and committing adultery both were punishable by death.

The fact that the punishment was local and temporary in no way affects the abiding place of the command. The only way to contradict this logic is to suggest that there is a difference between the fourth commandment and the other nine. All such attempts prove less than convincing. The "nine commandment party" argues that since the fourth commandment is never explicitly repeated in the New Testament, it cannot be regarded as authoritative for today's church. This fails to recognize the equal authority of the Old Testament and sidesteps the principle that whatever the Bible does not repeal remains in effect.[8] This does not mean that we fail to recognize that there are features of this Sabbath that are redundant. They are part of the ceremonial scaffolding that is dismantled as Christ fulfils the law. But although the scaffolding disappears, the building remains.

SABBATH, SUNDAY, LORD'S DAY

The relationship between the Old Testament Sabbath and the Lord's Day has been, through the years, the occasion of significant debate. Seventh Day Adventists have made this issue, if not the cornerstone of their system of belief, certainly their flagship. They are convinced that the church is commanded to observe the seventh day Sabbath. I regularly receive letters from radio listeners who are Seventh Day Adventists seeking to correct me on this issue. They are of the opinion that the early church continued to celebrate the Sabbath on the seventh day and that it was only when Constantine "interfered" that the day was changed to the first day of the week—the day in which the heathen worshiped the sun, hence Sunday.

This view is problematic to say the least. It assumes that there is a moral commandment laid upon us to keep the seventh day of the week. The vehemence with which this view is proclaimed is disproportionate to any biblical basis for it. We must discover whether the day itself is the vital element in the commandment or if the abiding moral obligation is that there should be six days of work followed by one day of rest.

From this perspective what is being mandated is that the divine pattern be followed. As God rested after six days of work, so His creatures set apart one day in seven expressly for rest and worship. "The Sabbath ordinance contained the positive law of one whole day in seven; that, from creation, was the seventh day. But the day may be changed without affecting the inherent moral character of the ordinance"[9] The Mosaic Sabbath was set within the framework of ceremonial laws which the first Christians soon realized had been fulfilled in the Lord Jesus and were no longer mandatory.

Paul addresses this in writing to the Colossians. "There-fore do not let anyone judge you by what you eat or drink, or with regard to a religious festival, a New Moon celebra-tion or a Sabbath day. These are a shadow of the things that were to come; the reality, however, is found in Christ" (Colossians 2:16–17). These verses, along with Romans 14:5–6 and Galatians 4:10–11, are pressed into service by those who argue for the redundancy of the fourth com-mandment. Paul is not setting aside the moral principle of sanctifying one day in seven. If in these verses Paul is setting aside a Sabbath, then it surely must be the seventh day Sab-bath with all of the Jewish ceremonies and shadows. (For a fuller discussion, see *The Lord's Day,* by Joseph A. Pipa.)

What, then, is the explanation for the change from Sat-urday to Sunday, from Sabbath to Lord's Day? Apart from Paul's use of the Jewish synagogue services as evangelistic opportunities, the last description of Christ's followers keeping the Jewish Sabbath is found at the end of Luke 23: "Then they went home and prepared spices and perfumes. But they rested on the Sabbath in obedience to the com-mandment." When they awakened the following morning to the fact of Christ's resurrection, everything was going to change!

> *It is a striking fact that the Jewish Sabbath almost disappears from recorded Christian practice after Christ's resurrection. The very day before his resurrection occurs, we find the disci-ples resting on the Jewish Sabbath, but after it has happened the observance of the seventh day is never mentioned except as a tolerated option for Jewish Christians (Romans 14:5), or an intolerable imposition by Judaizing heretics, or in passages where Paul reasoned with the Jews in the synagogue on the Sabbath, not apparently because the observance of the day is a*

regular part of his own devotional practise but because it pro-
vides an excellent opportunity for evangelism. [10]

The followers of Christ very quickly chose the first day
of the week as their special day when they would meet to
worship God. In doing so they were recognizing and establishing the significance of the Resurrection. Just as the deliverance from Egypt lay at the heart of the Mosaic Sabbath, so
the redemption accomplished by Christ is remembered on
the Lord's Day. While in principle every day is the Lord's
Day and may be the occasion of worship, the references to
the church's meeting "on the first day of the week" (Acts
20:7; 1 Corinthians 16:2) point to Sunday as the recognized
day of celebration and of rest.

When the apostle John refers to his being in the Spirit
on "the Lord's Day" (Revelation 1:10), the assumption is
that all his readers would understand the reference. The
change of day pointed to the shift in emphasis from the Old
Testament focus on creation and exodus from Egypt to the
New Testament memorial of Christ's work of re-creation and
the believer's liberation from the enslavement to sin. "If,
therefore, it had been appropriate to rest symbolically on
the Sabbath, the memorial of creation and deliverance from
the lesser bondage, it would surely have been regarded as
equally appropriate to rest symbolically on the Lord's Day,
the memorial of the new creation and deliverance from the
greater bondage."

Derek Prime provides a helpful summary when he
writes: "The change not only bore witness to the Resurrection, but it emphasized the difference between the Christian
Sunday and the Jewish Sabbath. The Jewish Sabbath came
at the end of six days and spoke of a rest to come; the Christian Sunday comes at the beginning of the week symbolis-

ing 'the rest' that Jesus Christ has won for those who trust Him."[11] I have been helped by thinking of the Lord's Supper as the memorial to His death and of the Lord's Day as the memorial to His resurrection. Once we have come to a deep conviction about the wonderful provision that God has made for us in this day, then we are in the position to think properly about what it means to keep the Lord's Day. By using *Sunday, Sabbath,* and *Lord's Day* interchangeably, we are simply affirming the abiding place of one day in seven for rest and worship.

OBSERVING THE SABBATH DAY

The command clearly states that we are to observe the Sabbath by "keeping it holy." The idea behind the word *holy* is that of being set apart from and for. One day in seven is set apart from the ordinary run of human activity for the express purpose of rest and worship. By means of our observance of the Lord's Day we "declare the praises of him who called you out of darkness into his wonderful light" (1 Peter 2:9). It should be no surprise, but rather, expected, that "a people belonging to God" should honor Him by delighting in this different day.

We are to cease from the work that has been our focus on the other six days. In other words, the ordinary routines of life are to be suspended not as an occasion for laziness but in order that we might ponder God's works, participate with His people in worship, and pursue opportunities to do good to others.

The Pharisees had no place in their system for works of piety or mercy. In the Talmud they devoted twenty-four chapters to the Sabbath. They had drawn up a catalogue of thirty-nine principal works, with six sub-categories, all of which were forbidden on the Sabbath. Their self-righteous, censorious attitude is clearly in evidence when they respond to the healing of the woman in the synagogue by saying, "There are six days for work. So come and be healed on those days, not on the Sabbath" (Luke 13:14). Jesus addressed their hypocrisy by pointing out that they had more care for their donkeys than for this "daughter of Abraham" (vv. 15–16).

That incident in the synagogue never fails to remind me of an occasion from my childhood. We had driven to the highlands of Scotland for a family vacation. As a result of a double booking, there was no room for us in the bed and breakfast where we had planned to stay. The following morning was Sunday, and our beleaguered little family was still searching for a place in which to stay for our two weeks of vacation. Arriving in Dornoch, we learned from the local police station (my father was a great believer in helpful friendly policemen) of possible accommodation in a cottage in the town. Since it was the Sabbath, we sat in the car waiting for the lady to return from morning worship.

When she appeared, my father stepped out to greet her. Although from inside the car we could not hear the conversation between them, it seemed clear to me from her "body language" that she was not excited about meeting my father! I was right. She told my father that she had no accommodation and that even if there were space available she would not give it to us because we were Sabbath-breakers, traveling on the Lord's Day! She assumed, wrongly, that we were traveling by choice rather than by necessity.

The story actually has a happy ending directly related to the Sabbath principle. Later that same day, we were welcomed into the home of another family. They were leaving the following morning for a two-week vacation and offered us their home in their absence. Their car was already packed ready for departure on the Monday. Their reason for not leaving on the Sunday was their conviction that since travel on that day was not a necessity they should not forsake the privilege and place of worship. Were it not for that commitment to the Lord's Day they would have been gone and we would never have been able to enjoy their hospitality, which was clearly an act of mercy!

In thinking of the negative response of the woman, John Murray's words ring loud and clear: "It is possible to make Sabbath-keeping, that is, abstinence from overt forms of desecration and attendance upon the exercises of worship, an instrument of the self-righteousness that is the arch-enemy of the Christian faith. This possibility is, I fear, too frequently an actuality."[12] A good question to ask in order to protect ourselves from pharisaical tendencies is this: "Does this activity promote the purposes of rest and worship?" Tasks which fall outside of the categories of works of necessity, mercy, and piety should be left for another day.

As we work through each of the commandments, we are helped by considering what the creeds and confessions have to say. The Heidelberg Catechism answers the question, "What does God require in the fourth commandment?" in this way:

First, the ministry of the Gospel and the schools be maintained; and that especially on the Sabbath, that is, on the day of rest, I diligently frequent the Church of God, to hear his word, to use the sacraments, publicly to call upon the Lord, and contribute to the relief of the poor as becomes a Christian. Secondly, that all the days of my life I cease from my evil works, and yield myself to the Lord, to work by his Holy Spirit in me: and thus begin in this life the eternal Sabbath.

This establishes the priority of the Lord's Day. This is in keeping with the emerging pattern of the church in the New Testament. "On the first day of the week we came together to break bread" (Acts 20:7). Although it is true that we may do this every day, Sunday provides a particular opportunity to enter into its benefits and to enjoy its privileges. It involves deliberately setting aside our own routine concerns for the express purpose of worship, fellowship, and acts of mercy. It is an opportunity to seek those things which are above and to care for our souls. Paul reminded Timothy that while physical fitness has a certain value, spiritual fitness is essential both for this life and for the life to come (1 Timothy 4:8). When a man refuses to miss his daily visit to the gym and yet neglects the gathering of God's people on the Lord's Day he is making a very clear statement about priorities.

For years now I have enjoyed the opportunity of taking Tuesday as a day off. I have purposefully referred to it as "Sue's Day," the point being that my focus and orientation on a Tuesday would be directly related to spending time with and enjoying the company of my wife. An outsider would have legitimate reason to doubt my heart's allegiance if I were to approach the day from a very selfish and legalistic perspective, for example, saying to myself, "If I can get my commitment over as quickly as possible, then I can have the rest of the time to myself." Then it would be a demand to be fulfilled rather than a delight to be enjoyed. It would also be possible to go to quite the other extreme and to wait for a surge of emotional intensity before spending time with her. Then it would be a hit-and-miss event, depending on one's feelings and the mood of the moment. It would be unrealistic to expect her to accept either approach.

Yet this is the way in which many believers approach the Lord's Day—either on the basis of legalistic, slavish drudgery or as a product of the ebb and flow of spiritual emotions. The first individual is often a gloomy character whose meticulous attendance, however brief, is divorced from an appreciation that Sabbath observance is an abomination to the Lord when divorced from redeeming, regenerating, and sanctifying grace. The second individual fails to understand that duty and delight are not protagonists. He never does what he should until he feels right about it, and consequently his attendance at worship is a victim of his emotions rather than a servant of his will. When a congregation of God's people comes to a deep-seated conviction about the precious priority of the Lord's Day, when they call the Sabbath a delight, and when they rejoice in the instruction of God's Word and the fellowship of God's people, then other considerations and obligations, appetites and preoccupations will become secondary to this great priority.

When I was a student I purposefully chose not to study on a Sunday. As a result I enjoyed tremendous freedom on the Lord's Day. I was able to attend the morning service, accept invitations to lunch and tea, and enjoy the privilege of evening worship without feeling that I was neglecting my studies. As a by-product I found that it caused me to organize my time and be more productive during the rest of the week. I often challenge students to try this approach and to discover what will happen when they restructure their lives around the "fixed point" of the priority of the Lord's Day.

Consider what a difference there will be when the people of God decide to do something so simple, sensible, and biblical as making their participation in the regular worship services of their church a priority. Imagine the impact of church families framing the Lord's Day with morning and evening worship. Instead of simply making phones ring in political protest, why don't we commit to making the church bells ring in joyful timely reminder of the Creator's lordship over time and of the Redeemer's victory over sin.

Those who argue against such an emphasis by claiming that every day is the Lord's Day face the challenge of making every day look like Sunday rather than what is usually the case—Sunday now looks like every other day. The choice is plain. Either we determine to move to the rhythm of the saints or we will march to the drumbeat of the world. "When Sunday is swallowed up by the weekend and loses its uniqueness, its holiness, as the Lord's Day, then you and I are the inevitable losers. We cannot, by taking shortcuts, gain what the Sabbath was designed to give us. McSabbath may satisfy the immediate itch, but it cannot satisfy our souls."[13]

When we begin to view the Lord's Day in light of principle, then the questions of procedure are less likely to trip us up. For example, once the family has decided that worshiping together on the Lord's Day is a non-negotiable for them, they will not have to continually debate the questions that arise concerning sports and recreation. If a family does not establish corporate worship as a fixed point, then worship will have to fight for a place on the schedule along with swim team, travel soccer, band practice, and sleepovers. Once the principle is in place, then exceptions can be addressed by learning to ask the right questions.

- Is this activity a selfish indulgence?
- Am I just doing as I please without reference to God and His Word?
- Will participation be a help or a hindrance to delighting in the Sabbath?
- Am I helping others to take the Lord's Day seriously by engaging in this activity?

In all of this we mustn't forget that God has provided this Sabbath for our well-being and enjoyment. God is gracious in making provision for us in a day of rest and worship. He is worthy of our exclusive devotion.

There can be little doubt that God's people would once again make a dramatic impact on our culture if we were to make a serious attempt to enjoy the weekly rest in preparation for the eternal rest which awaits us (Hebrews 4:9). There should be about our weekly Sabbaths a foretaste of the ultimate delight that will be ours one day in heaven. Those of us who are responsible for the conduct of worship and the preaching of the Good News dare not evade the responsibility to see to it that our gatherings are marked by reverential joy rather than by heaviness and dreary routine. Listen to Isaiah on this subject:

> If you keep your feet from breaking the Sabbath
>> and from doing what you please on my holy day,
> if you call the Sabbath a delight
>> and the Lord's holy day honorable,
> and if you honor it by not going your own way
>> and not doing as you please or speaking idle words,
> then you will find your joy in the LORD,
>> and I will cause you to ride on the heights of the land
>> and to feast on the inheritance of your father Jacob.
>> The mouth of the Lord has spoken.
>> —ISAIAH 58:13–14

On the strength of this proclamation my parents taught me this simple rhyme:

A Sunday well spent

Brings a week of content,

113

And strength for the toils of tomorrow.

But a Sunday profaned

Whatever is gained,

Is a certain forerunner for sorrow.

5

FAMILY LIFE— GOD'S WAY

Honor your father and your mother, so that you may live long in the land the LORD your God is giving you.

—EXODUS 20:12

$\mathcal{T}$homas Hazard was a fifth-generation American and a son of Robert Hazard, one of many Rhode Island landowners who used the labor of slaves in the 1700s to amass great fortune. Robert Hazard was also highly influential in church and government. As Thomas grew, he understood that he was destined to follow in his father's footsteps, inheriting land, wealth, and power.

Then, as a young man, Thomas experienced a deep conversion to Christ, which led him to a sincere conviction that it was against God's law to enslave other human beings. With a small band of other young Christian men, Thomas drafted petitions that asked New England's slaveholders, including his own father, to free their slaves.

The slaveholders were outraged. Moreover, the young men's fathers felt humiliated and betrayed. How could their own sons dishonor them in the eyes of their peers, questioning their moral and spiritual bearing? Anathemas were pronounced. Wills were torn up and re-drawn. Some sons were banished forever from their families.

Facing his father's fiery judgment, Thomas humbly asked for his forgiveness. He had acted out of conviction but also without thought for his father's honor. He could not change his conviction, he said, but he would do whatever else he could to restore all the honor justly due to his father.

Whether it was the tenderness of the son's genuine apology, or his tactful diplomacy, or the strong, steady manliness of Christ that shone in him at that moment, the father's heart was moved. How could a father fail to be won over by such a humble and respectful son?

Father and son remained close, even though they were on opposite sides of the slave-holding issue. And although Robert kept slaves throughout his life, he made provision, in accordance with his son's convictions, to free those that were still being held at the time of his death.

Thomas and his friends went on to win over the New England colonial legislatures to the antislavery position and helped draft the laws prohibiting slavery that would be enacted when those colonies became states after the American Revolution. Through Thomas, the Hazard family gained distinction and honor for being among the first white Americans to fight the evil of slavery. It is also said that throughout his life Robert, though reluctant to join his son's cause, was secretly proud of his son's work and for having produced "a man of such strong convictions."

Though unable to compromise his spiritual stance, Thomas brought honor to his father and his family.

Perhaps you think it odd to begin a chapter about honoring your parents with the story of a young man who publicly embarrassed his father and opposed the way he acquired his wealth. Many would ask: "How could he honor his father while seeing the wrong his father was doing?" But that is not the right question, although it is the way most would phrase it today: "How can I honor my father when he drinks, or is mean and abusive, or is a bigot?" "How can I honor my mother when she has always been self-involved, caught up in her career and hobbies and friends?" "How can I honor my parents when they have never had much interest in me?"

But for Thomas Hazard the question was: "How can I see the wrong my father is doing and still find a way to honor him? How can I obey God's fifth commandment?"

WHAT'S BECOME OF FATHER AND MOTHER?

Parental authority is indispensable to a stable society. Through the ages, virtually all civilizations have recognized this truth. From the beginning, God placed mankind in families, establishing this relational unit as the building block of society. Parents were to be responsible for their children, and children were to submit to the authority of their parents. This natural law finds expression in the fifth commandment of God's revealed Law. It is no exaggeration to say that the well-being of a person, people, or nation begins in the home. A home in which a father and a mother function together in fulfilling the responsibility to train up their children in the way they should go. With this context, beliefs and values are transmitted from one generation to another.

It is no secret that this "traditional" family unit is under attack. It's a place a variety of family forms are offered as viable and acceptable alternatives. The family is God's design. He has established the coming together of one man and one woman in a lifelong commitment. Immoral associations between people of the same sex violate God's Law.

In 1995 an article entitled "Promoting No Dad Families" appeared in *U.S. News and World Report*. It addressed the question: "Why isn't there some debate about the fact that American sperm banks sell sperm to single women?" Given that no-father children, as a group, are at risk in all races and at all income levels, shouldn't society have an interest in discouraging the intentional creation of fatherless children? European guidelines, produced by the Council of Europe in 1989, say that sperm should be made available only to heterosexual couples. But in America, where at least three thousand fatherless babies are produced each year through artificial insemination, little serious moral debate has occurred.

The reason is clear. The feminist, homosexual agenda, in seeking to legitimize itself, demands the "right" to establish a family in any way it chooses. The reproductive "rights" of women have so dominated the discussion of procreation issues that the part played by fathers has been almost totally ignored. "In an age of antagonism between the sexes, it's a short step to the view of fathers as troublesome, marginal and essentially irrelevant inseminators." This confusion and corruption is a large part of the social landscape in which we are called to obey the fifth commandment.

The apostle Paul described in a catalogue of views the dreadful decline of a culture when it turns its back on God to worship the creature rather than the Creator. "They are full of envy, murder, strife, deceit and malice. They are gossips, slanderers, God-haters, insolent, arrogant and boastful; they invent ways of doing evil; they disobey their parents; they are senseless, faithless, heartless, ruthless" (Romans 1:29–31). He reminds Timothy of the same. People will love themselves and money rather than love God. Instead of humbly acknowledging the mess in which they find themselves, they will be conceited, abusive, lacking in natural affection and (here it comes again) *disobedient to their parents.* It is a picture of a culture lying like a broken-down tour bus on the side of the freeway. Smoke billows from under the hood, the axles are snapped, and the wheels are off. The travelers offer a variety of suggestions for getting it going. Somehow they are reluctant to reach for the owner's manual! Is this not where we are? With the basic unit of stable society struggling for its life there is still a reluctance to turn to the manual of the Bible. "Through this gate," we can say, "is the pathway to freedom."

We noted earlier that the Ten Commandments give practical expression to the great summary statement made by Jesus upon which all the Law and the prophets hang: "Love the Lord your God. . . . Love your neighbor as yourself" (Matthew 22:37, 39).

It is common to think of the two tables of the Law containing four and six commands respectively, the first four addressing love for God, and the remaining six, love for our neighbor. Jewish scholars tended to divide them five and five. In doing so, they included the honoring of parents under our duty to God. This makes sense. How could we ever claim to honor God, whom we have not seen, if we fail to honor our parents, whom we do see? Parental authority is divinely delegated and is an integral part of our reverence for God.

God is very serious about this. His call to holy living in Leviticus 19:1–2 is immediately followed by the statement, "Each of you must respect his mother and father" (v. 3). The death penalty was to be pronounced upon those who cursed their parents. Although we do not face the same penalty, the place God gives to honoring our parents has not changed. The great need for this command is to be found in the fact that we are by nature, rebels. We have a natural dislike for authority. It is within the family that children are to learn respect for authority.

HONOR TO WHOM HONOR IS DUE

When a parent exclaims to a child, "You don't treat me with an ounce of respect," he is chiding that child for a lack of honor. *Honor* is a "weighty" word. The Hebrew word *kabed* means "to be heavy." So to honor our parents is to treat them, we might say, with a ton of respect! The Greek equivalent of the Hebrew word, used in the New Testament, *timao,* extends the thought to placing a high value upon them.

My children are amused because I take such interest in a television program called *Antiques Roadshow.* You have to be a bit of an antique yourself to really enjoy it. Furniture, porcelain, and paintings are produced by members of the public. Great excitement is experienced vicariously by the viewer when someone discovers that a tea set, which has been around forever, is worth a great deal of money. In a similar way it often takes children considerable time to realize the huge value of their parents' instruction and discipline. This fifth commandment establishes the fact that our parents are, by God's design, to be revered and that the honor we give them is to be a reflection of the honor we ought to give to God our heavenly Father. No child, no family, no church, no city, no country or people will ever give honor where honor is due and respect where respect is required unless they are taught respect, honor, and obedience within their homes and for their parents.

Teaching the Parents

How can we possibly expect children to know their boundaries when the parents themselves are clueless about their responsibilities? Growing up as I did in the 1950s, the parental maxim "Children should be seen and not heard" was accepted and applied. Despite claims to the contrary, it doesn't seem to have produced a generation of cowering, uncommunicative social misfits. But it is we, the baby boomers, who are accused of raising the most spoiled generation ever. The pendulum has swung way past the center. The mantra of the moment is "My child is going to be seen and heard."

Those of us who have had the back of our seat kicked by a three-year-old from Los Angeles to Chicago were quickly alerted to our predicament when we heard Daddy in the row behind "reasoning" with his three-year-old monster about the merits and demerits of kicking the gentleman's chair intermittently throughout an entire airplane flight! We have all had occasion to groan at least inwardly as a foursome of young mothers accompanied by their offspring arrive just at lunch time to tyrannize the restaurant. Without the "rod of correction," they sit in embarrassed silence as their children hold them to emotional ransom. The children are not corrected, directed, or ejected. Instead they are encouraged to speak their minds, and every parental "request" becomes a matter of negotiation. Since Lucian is never enthusiastic about getting into the tub, his parents seek to cajole him. "We like him to take a bath every night, but sometime it's not worth the fight."

The cover story of an August 2001 editorial in *Time* magazine asked the question: "Do kids have too much power?" The article began:

Here is a parenting parable for our age. Carla Wagnar, 17, of Coral Gables, FL, spent the afternoon drinking the tequila she charged on her American Express Gold card before speeding off in her high performance Audi A4. She was dialing her cell phone when she ran over Helen Marie Witty, a 16-year-old student who was out rollerblading. Charged with drunken driving and manslaughter, Carla was given a trial date—at which point her parents asked the judge whether it would be okay if Carla went ahead and spent the summer in Paris as she usually does.

If this seems extreme, consider this: One of my daughters applied for a position as a nanny in the home of an educated, well-to-do family in Santa Barbara, California. The terms were highly attractive: only one child to care for, live-in quarters, a car, and a monthly salary that would more than cover student costs. Michelle didn't take the job. She removed herself from the running when the mother informed her that if she were to become the nanny, she could never say no to the child. She could distract the child but was never to deny it. What chance do the children have when the parents are so sadly clueless or willfully foolish? In contrast to the chaos that results from such confused thinking, the Bible provides clear instruction that we neglect to our peril.

CHILDREN ARE GIFTS FROM GOD

In the prologue to the marriage service, the minister reminds the couple that they must enter this union thoughtfully, considering the purposes for which God established it. It was established for the welfare of human society; the life-long companionship and help the husband and wife are to give to each other; and the continuance of family life as God intended, that children, who are gifts from the Lord, should be carefully brought up and trained to love and obey God. The story of the birth of Samuel records the reaction of Hannah to the privilege of parenting: "I prayed for this child, and the LORD has granted me what I asked of him. So now I give him to the LORD" (1 Samuel 1:27–28).

Every gift the Lord gives, including our children, should not be selfishly retained but instead generously shared. Above all, parents should want their children to grow up like Samuel, to love and serve God. This involves training them in the way they should go and being clear about what's expected.

INSTRUCTION STARTS AT HOME

Whatever choice parents make about the ongoing education of their children, they are responsible for the instruction of their children in the Law of God from their earliest days. Paul warns fathers about exasperating their children and directs them to "bring them up in the training and instruction of the Lord" (Ephesians 6:4). The Shema (*Shama'*, Hebrew for "hear," Deuteronomy 6:4–9) gives guidance on how this may be achieved. The commands of God are first to be upon the parents' hearts so that they are not merely providing head knowledge. They are to impress them upon the children in the context of everyday family life.

The picture is not one of formal instruction but the kind of learning that takes place as the family travels, lies down for the night, and rises to the opportunities and demands of a new day. In this way, a child begins to develop a biblical-walk view without even realizing. After we have said their prayers with them, in those precious moments before sleep takes them away, we are confronted with such questions as,

"Where was I before I was born?" We need to be ready to tell them: "You did not exist before you were conceived. You were created uniquely by God and given to your mom and dad as a gift, and we're so thankful."

The child nurtured by a biblical view of life's origin will enjoy a security that can't be shared by the youngster schooled in evolutionary theory, which is forced to inform him that he exists as a matter of time plus matter plus chance. Susan and I found that it was often when we were lying down at the end of the day or driving on a vacation that we were able to help our children work through questions raised in their local elementary school. It would seem the task is never complete. Even now, our adult children are ready to receive instruction from their elders. What a privilege for a young man to be able to concur with Solomon's words:

> When I was a boy in my father's house,
> still tender, and an only child of my mother,
> he taught me and said,
> "Lay hold of my words with all your heart;
> keep my commands and you will live."
> —PROVERBS 4:3–4

DISCIPLINE IS NOT AN OPTION

It is absolutely essential that parents do not shirk their God-given responsibilities. One of the characteristics required in the elders who lead the church is the effective management of home life. "He must manage his own family well and see that his children obey him with proper respect" (1 Timothy 3:4). This is a responsibility in which both husband and wife share. It is vital that they present a united front because children are quickly very adept at trying to play one parent off against the other. The social and political climate is one in which the "rights" of the child have been set out in such a way as to severely inhibit the parental exercise of discipline. In seeking to uphold and apply the biblical guidelines, we face the charge of being hateful toward our children. Nothing could be farther from the truth. Indeed, such a suggestion turns truth on its head. The exercise of discipline is motivated by the kind of love that longs to prevent our children from reaching the end of their lives on the brink of ruin because they hated discipline, spurned correction, and paid no attention to their teachers. The real "hatred" is expressed in a failure to discipline: "He who spares the rod hates his son, but he who loves him is careful to discipline him" (Proverbs 13:24).

If parents do not quickly establish this framework, the challenge will become greater with every day of neglect. The foolishness that is bound up in the heart of a child will take more than words to dislodge. The dreadful accounts of parents whose vicious tempers have erupted in the physical abuse of their children should serve as a warning to all. However, such accounts cannot be used to set aside the necessary, controlled, and God-ordained corporal discipline of our children. In my experience as both child and parent, it is clear that one well-positioned rap from a wooden spoon was more effective than a thousand words. Very quickly the spoon only needs to "appear" in order to bring about the desired effect. We are not surprised that many of our secular neighbors oppose these views and are afraid to discipline their children. What I find most alarming is the negative reaction of the "Christian" counselor to the father who made use of the following letter in seeking to establish guidelines for his son. The counselor was apparently enraged by the very idea.

Dear Son:

As long as you live under this roof you will follow the rules. In our house we do not have a democracy. I did not campaign to be your father. You did not vote for me. We are father and son by the grace of God. I consider it a privilege and I accept the responsibility. In accepting it, I have an obligation to perform the role of a father. I am not your pal. The age difference makes such a relationship impossible. We can share many things, but you must remember that I'm your father. This is 100 times more meaningful than being a pal. You will do as I say as long as you live in this house. You are not to disobey me, because whatever I ask you to do is motivated by love. This may be hard for you to understand at times, but the rule holds. You will understand perfectly when you have a son of your own. Until then, trust me.

Love, Dad

This letter is not a perfect expression of what's involved, but it does issue a strong call to take seriously the child's duty to honor his parents.

GOD EXPECTS EVERY CHILD TO DO HIS DUTY

Do you recall the quote from Admiral L. Nelson with which we began? It is safe to suggest that those sailors submitted to the authority of the admiral, having learned the pattern of submission first within the home. Learning how to respond to authority takes place as we submit to our parents as the first and most basic God-given authority on earth. "Listen to your father, who gave you life, and do not despise your mother when she is old. . . . The father of a righteous man has great joy; he who has a wise son delights in him. May your father and mother be glad; may she who gave you birth rejoice!" (Proverbs 23:22, 24–25).

Discipline

We honor our parents by submitting to their discipline. It is the fool who spurns his father's discipline. The fact that we are on the receiving end of our father's discipline is actually a privilege and an advantage because it produces a harvest. Although the immediate experience is not pleasant but painful, in the long run we enjoy the benefits of the righteousness of peace. We can think of this discipline in two ways. One is the discipline of correction, which is intended to drive out faults. In submitting to this discipline we say, "I agree with you that what I did was wrong. I am sorry. I accept my punishment." The other is the discipline of training, which teaches us skills that are useful and necessary in life. In response to this we say, "I agree that learning this particular skill will help me in my life. I accept your instruction."

When a child resents and rejects parental discipline and is not "trained by it," he begins to develop emotional calluses. He grows increasingly antagonistic toward all kinds of authority and will in the end become a menace to society and himself.

Love

The Bible takes for granted the natural affection between parent and child. Jesus warns against the strength of these natural ties taking priority over a man or a woman's love for Him. This love is not slushy or sentimental, but neither is it devoid of emotion. It will express itself in different ways depending upon the age and circumstances of the child. In the teenage years when a young man is in the company of his peers, he is far less likely to make a public display of affection for his parents. Ironically, the same individual may be perfectly happy to publicly display his affection for a girlfriend.

However love is conveyed, it must be sincere. The last time I saw my father before he died, we talked together about life's comings and goings. He was the patient in a hospital bed being treated for heart failure, and I was the visitor. Neither of us on that evening had any reason to believe that we were in each other's company for the last time this side of heaven. During several months it had not been uncommon for him to be admitted to the hospital so that they could monitor and balance his medication. As I stood up to leave, I thought how best to display my love for my father. We routinely shook hands or hugged, but we hadn't kissed since my early teens. As I bent to kiss him on the cheek, he turned his head and we kissed lips to lips in what was to be my final public demonstration of love for him. I'm glad we did. The memory is precious.

Obedience

Love and obedience go hand in hand. In providing rules for Christian households, Paul instructs the Colossians, "Children, obey your parents in everything, for this pleases the Lord" (Colossians 3:20). Note the comprehensive nature of this command. Children are not to be selective in their obedience, choosing to obey only when it suits them. Assuming that the parents are making no illegitimate demands, the children are to be wholehearted in bowing to their authority.

Real obedience is a matter of the heart. Sadly, it is possible to cultivate a spirit of reluctant, external subservience that is only a thin disguise for a stubborn and rebellious heart. We must resist the temptation to despise their directives while appearing to comply. It's like the small boy who resisted his mother's request for him to sit down in the back of the car. Twice she asked him to sit, and he remained standing. Her third request was accompanied by a swat on his defiant little knees. He was seated but declared: "I may be sitting down on the outside, but I'm standing up on the inside."

Respect

In the Southern states it is still quite common to hear children respond to questions from their parents with a "Yes, sir," or a "No, ma'am." While this may be nothing more than custom and may not represent the heart attitude, it is still to be preferred to the disrespectful responses of so many young people. To respect our parents means speaking kindly to them and about them. We make our reverence for them apparent not only by our words but also with our eyes. We have all watched a youngster speaking to his parents by phone. We can tell from the expression in his eyes whether his attitude is represented in his words. Respect demands that we look into our parents' eyes as we address them. I still have a very vivid picture of my wife taking our son's little face in her hands and inclining his gaze toward her. "Let me see your eyes," she would say.

Solomon uses a startling image with respect to this, "The eye that mocks a father, that scorns obedience to a mother, will be pecked out by the ravens of the valley, will be eaten by the vultures" (Proverbs 30:17).

Charles Bridges comments: "Observe the guilt only of a scornful look, or the mocking eye, when perhaps not a word is spoken. Certainly if the fifth commandment is 'the first with promise,' it is also the first with judgment. No commandment in the breach of it is visited with more tremendous threatenings. Pride comes before destruction."[1]

We must beware of criticizing, mocking, or insulting our parents. Many a hardened criminal will confess that their first step on the road to their sorry end was contempt of parental authority and restraint.

Devotion

We are living in an aging population. People are living longer and are increasingly in need of care. While the church has a responsibility to care for the elderly, children and grandchildren must practice their religion by "caring for their own family and so repaying their parents and grandparents, for this is pleasing to God" (1 Timothy 5:4). By obeying this command, the believer has the opportunity to shine in the darkness.

Twelve years ago *Newsweek* magazine was reporting on a disturbing trend of turning hospitals into a "dumping grounds for granny." Thirty-eight percent of hospitals responding to a survey by the Senate Committee on Aging reported, "As many as eight elderly patients get dumped on their emergency wards every week." When surveyed, barely half of the American public believed it was the children's responsibility to look after their parents.

The fifth commandment calls us to be the best visitors of our elderly and infirm, the most willing to provide accommodations, and the most prepared to uphold the place of maturity and old age. This is not a popular doctrine in the twenty-first century, where youth is worshiped and old age dreaded and despised. Old age is viewed at best as a relief from the grind of having to get up in the morning and at worst as an existence that offers no reason to get up at all.

The pressing relevance of this command is impossible to miss in a society that isolates and impoverishes its elderly and flirts with euthanasia as a viable solution for all. To honor our parents is to care for them as age takes its long, slow, inevitable toll. It is to stand by them at all times in genuine love. Not a sporadic, "when it's convenient" love, or a greeting card mushy sentimental love, but a sustained love that is forbearing, patient, and quick to forgive.

EXCEPTIONS, EXAMPLES, PROMISE

Are there limits to the jurisdiction of parents? Clearly the answer is yes. If parents were to command their children to do anything that contravenes God's Law, then the apostles' provide us with the answer: "We must obey God rather than men!" (Acts 5:29). Paul reminded his readers that their obedience to their parents was "in the Lord" (Ephesians 6:1). Parents' authority is not universal; they may only require obedience in such things as fit within the framework of the Lord's authority.

Parents may not overstep the new boundaries set by the leaving and cleaving of marriage. The husband-wife relationship takes priority over the relationship that was previously enjoyed with the parents. This change in priority demands no lessening of affection or care.

If you find yourself in the course of considering all these biblical principles asking "I wonder what this looks like," let me suggest the story of Joseph. His devotion to his father was undiminished by time and distance. His first question after disclosing himself to his brothers was, "Is my father still living?" (Genesis 45:3). His provision for his father is his earliest thought. "Hurry back to my father and say to him, . . . "Come down to me, don't delay. . . . I will provide for you" (vv. 9, 11). His affection for his father was so deep that it could not be contained when they were reunited: "He threw his arms around his father and wept for a long time" (Genesis 46:29). His admiration for his father is seen in the obvious pride with which he presents him to Pharaoh and in the generous settlement he made available to him (Genesis 47:7, 11). Each of these factors is present in Joseph's obedient actions as he oversees the embalming and burial of Jacob. With an eye to detail, he honors his father not only in his presence but also in his absence.

One summer Sunday evening when we had held our service outdoors, I met a visiting family. They had brought with them their elderly grandmother who, on her next birthday, would be one hundred years old. She was a lovely lady, alert and interesting, and I took the opportunity to introduce my children to her (it's not every Sunday evening one meets an centenarian!).

As we were driving home together, one of our children said, "That lady must have really honored her mom and dad!" This promise is not categorized, or given to individuals. It is rather a general promise given to the society that adopts the principle. We all know obedient children who died young, and we know disobedient children who have grown old. So the principle in the promise is this: Children who are taught to obey God by honoring their parents will grow up to be responsible citizens. And responsible citizens make for a strong nation. So let us honor our parents as we respectfully seek their advice and wisdom, as we value their guidance about friends, schooling, employment, marriage, child rearing, life and aging and eternity, and God. They are ahead of us on their pathway—a pathway to freedom.

6

LIFE IS SACRED

You shall not murder.
—EXODUS 20:13

$\mathcal{T}$his sixth commandment comes to us in four simple words: "You shall not murder." The original Hebrew records it even more simply: "No murder." It condemns the deliberate, malicious, and unlawful taking of life.

In 1963, in Scotland, two people were convicted of murder. In 2000, there were 128 recorded homicides. In 1960 the District of Columbia reported 81 murders. In 1991 there were 482, and in 2000 the figure was 239.[1] In the nation's capital people are being murdered at the rate of more than four per week. Apparently, when it comes to the sixth commandment, something has been lost in the translation! Life is apparently going cheap. This command declares life is sacred.

Most people would agree that getting angry, pulling a gun, and shooting someone in cold blood is wrong. Beyond this, however, matters of life and death sometimes get a bit hazy. What if someone is terminally ill? Can we "assist" him on his way? What if someone is elderly and ill and has few resources available for her care? Isn't euthanasia the merciful and compassionate way out? What if a woman is pregnant through rape or incest? Or what if an expected child is likely to be handicapped? In those cases, isn't abortion the best alternative?

Christians and non-Christians alike have become hotly embroiled in legal and political squabbles over such issues as euthanasia and abortion. Yet how many have considered, in the privacy of their own hearts, where they stand in relation to the sixth commandment? Our Western democratic governments, together with modern philosophies, have so vigorously promoted the sovereignty, sacredness, and rights of the individual—with a strong emphasis on personal rights—that they have forgotten the One from whom those rights derive.

THE AUTHOR OF LIFE

Fundamental to this sixth commandment, as with all the commandments, is the existence of a personal Creator God. Because God is, the universe and all within it exists, and only God has the ultimate authority over His creation: "I AM . . . therefore, you shall." God the Creator stands behind the universe, providing its ultimate source of meaning.

Of all God's created things, however, one has been given special honor and distinction, and that is mankind. We alone, of all creation, have been made in God's image. We owe our existence to the existence of a God who personally and purposefully created us in His own image, establishing a continuity between our finite selves and His infinite Self and giving our lives unique dignity and value.

As God is always reflected and revealed in His creation,

so He is reflected and revealed in us. Or, to put it another way, we are small reflections of His divine glory. The very "manishness of man," said Francis Schaeffer, attests to our distinction from the rest of God's created order. Our creativity, our sense of justice and morality, our self-awareness, our ability to communicate and use the power of language, our minds, and our never-dying soul are all evidences that we are made in God's image.

God is the infinite Creator, the author of life. He spoke . . . and the world came into being. He spoke . . . and the authority of His Law was established. Behind this sixth commandment, "You shall not murder," lies the authority of the Creator God.

THE HOSTILITY OF MAN

Since Adam and Eve's original act of sin in the Garden of Eden, man's reaction to authority can be summed up in one word: hostility. This is aptly summarized by Paul in Romans 8, where, in the course of a wider argument, he makes it clear that the natural man—that is, the unregenerate, sinful man—is hostile to God. "The mind of sinful man is death, but the mind controlled by the Spirit is life and peace; the sinful mind is hostile to God. It does not submit to God's law, nor can it do so. Those controlled by the sinful nature cannot please God" (vv. 6–8).

Sinful men and women cannot tolerate the idea that God is in control. Rather than acknowledging God's creative work and submitting to His Law, they would rather believe that the universe just happened, a result of chance events somewhere in time. A God who is nonexistent, irrelevant, or dead can demand nothing. In the words of folk artist Joan Baez, we "are the orphans in an age of no tomorrows."[2]

Begin with some impersonal force, add the passage of time and a number of chance occurrences, and, "Welcome to a meaningless, absurd universe."

Perhaps filmmaker and actor Woody Allen expressed this worldview best. Allen may be a filmmaking genius, but he is also one of the saddest popular philosophers of our time. In the film *Annie Hall,* in what is supposed to be a humorous line, Allen says, "Mankind is left with alienation, loneliness, and an emptiness verging on madness. . . . Life is divided into the horrible and the miserable."

The billboards on the postmodern road of life read: "You are going nowhere." "You have no reason to exist." Read today's headlines and you will see how far down this road most of society has gone. "Mother Drowns Her Own Children When Boyfriend Rejects Her." "Son Shoots Elderly, Ailing Parents." "Teenager Abandons Newborn in Dumpster."

Why? Because modern men and women, in their human hostility toward God, have rejected the Maker's instructions.

Before he tried to commit suicide, artist Paul Gauguin scrawled on his final painting, "Whence come we, what are we, wither do we go?"

The answer of modern man?

"Where do we come from?"

"Nowhere."

"What are we?"

"Nothing."

"Where are we going?"

"No place."

P.S.: Have a nice life.

We cannot overstate how important it is for us to recognize the vast difference between believing all is chance and believing that our lives have been created by a personal, purposeful, involved, and loving God. Follow these two roads to their logical conclusion and you will quickly see the fundamental distinction between the believer and the unbeliever.

We may live next door to each other, share an office, play on the same softball team, and listen to the same music, but spiritually we are worlds apart. What is important, though, is not just to recognize that we are different but to understand why our thinking is different and to be able to give a reasonable explanation for the truth about God and life and the value of life.

Being pro-life must be more than a flippant statement on our bumper sticker or a way to cast our vote. It must be a studied position we hold with all the energy of our convictions. This is hard work. As we saw earlier, the postmodern mind-set is such that, as Colson says, "We must challenge its false presuppositions, lovingly explaining that there is truth and that it is knowable."

Only a firm set of principles, expressive of a biblical worldview, provides an adequate reason to value life. This then provides the substantive basis for exalting the sanctity of life and seeking to correct those who would devalue human existence.

When it becomes a hardship to care for Grandma, when a baby may be born severely handicapped, when more tax money is required to support the infirm or afflicted, the logical choice will seem obvious. In short, when we base our position on emotion, pragmatism, or even radicalism without roots, the choice will always favor whatever we can talk ourselves into feeling comfortable with at a given moment, depending on the pressure of circumstances. And in the end, the latent hostility to the authority of God that lies within each of us is likely to win the day.

THE SANCTITY OF LIFE

Only on the basis of the Word of God can we establish the sacredness of life. The Bible says life is sacred because it is God's gift. Human life is the most precious thing in all the world, and to end it or direct its ending is God's prerogative alone. We honor God by respecting His image in each of us, which means preserving and furthering each other's welfare at all times. This life-honoring ethos lies behind the command, "You shall not murder."

Unfortunately, since mankind is hostile to the authority of God and His truth, we flagrantly violate this commandment in several ways.

Homicide

Each day across this land and around the world men, women, and children are shot, stabbed, and beaten to death. Drive-by shootings are a common occurrence in our cities. In Los Angeles they throw pipe bombs through car windows. Children shoot other children on the school playground.

Abuse, abduction, and torture have become commonplace. In Liverpool, England, eleven- and twelve-year-old boys lured a three-year-old away from his mother in a shopping center and beat him before dumping him to die on a railway line.

Children used to be able to play peacefully and safely in their own neighborhoods. Now we must have neighborhood watches to protect them—and sometimes even that is not enough. Many children are not even safe in their own homes.

We have broken the link between a personal God and

His creation. We have dismantled the Bible and considered life meaningless and absurd. Behind a façade of worldly wisdom we have become foolish. With our own hands we have torn down humanity, and we are left with the tragic result: violence against our own kind and the willful destruction of human life. When we break the link between a personal Creator God and His creation, life becomes worthless.

But a word of warning here. We are sickened by brutal killers like Charles Manson and Jeffrey Dahmer. Our minds recoil from the pictures and descriptions of their heinous crimes. Yet men and women flock by the millions to be "entertained" by gruesome movies such as *Silence of the Lambs*. We routinely watch television shows depicting the most hideous sorts of violence. By the time our young children enter school, they may have already witnessed several thousand murders, shootings, stabbings, or beatings on television.

Why have we, as Christians, allowed ourselves to be drawn in by forces that find the destruction of sacred human life entertaining? The fact that we have done so is the real measure of the depth to which our whole culture has sunk.

Suicide/Euthanasia

Ask the locals in Waterford Township, Michigan, about Polson Street. They call it "the Road of Death," because it is there that a man by the name of Kevorkian enabled fifteen or more people to usurp God's role and take their own lives. Kevorkian himself has more than once expressed his egoistic and nihilistic worldview. "Everyone is a phony"—everyone except him. "Doctors are socially criminal. Legislators are barbarians and church officials are religious fanatics. You don't see the tragedies. What are we doing? Nobody cares." Therefore, he says, "Put on this death mask and all will be well."

I have in front of me as I write a list of the names of ninety-three individuals who were assisted by Dr. Jack Kevorkian, a retired pathologist, in taking their own lives. The youngest name on the list is that of Roosevelt Dawson. He was a twenty-one-year-old suffering from quadriplegia. According to Kevorkian's lawyer, this list is made up of the deaths recorded in the newspapers. There have been many other murders that have been kept private. Kevorkian is currently in jail, describing himself as a "prisoner of conscience" and "martyr to the cause of the right to choose to die." The Euthanasia Research and Guidance Organization (ERGO) support him. Their president, Derek Humphrey said: "Kevorkian's martyrdom—self-imposed as it is—will speed up the day when voluntary euthanasia for the dying is removed from the legal classification of 'murder' and recognized as a justifiable act of compassion."[3]

It is distinctly possible that other countries, including the United States, will follow The Netherlands in legalizing euthanasia. No matter how it may read on the statute books of man, it will remain murder on the statute of God's Law.

The American Hospital Association has estimated that some 70 percent of the six thousand deaths that occur in U.S. hospitals each day are the result of someone deciding they want further treatment withheld. Some doctors routinely give their dying patients the means to take their own lives. Dr. John Flaxner, a Vanderbilt Medical School professor who teaches on death, dying, and bereavement, says, "If a terminal patient wants to die there is a way he can help. I say, 'I'm giving you this prescription medicine and this sleeping pill. For God's sake don't ever take them together . . . because that would kill you.'"

Suicide is becoming an epidemic in our culture. The offices of counselors and pastors are flooded with suffering people seeking help from anyone who can save them from self-destruction.

Suicide is the ninth leading cause of death in the U.S., with 31,204 deaths recorded in 1995. This approximates to around one death every seventeen minutes. There are more suicides than homicides each year in the United States. From 1952 to 1992, the incidence of suicide among teens and young adults tripled.[4] Today it is the third leading cause of death for teenagers aged fifteen to nineteen (after motor vehicle accidents and unintentional injury). Suicide is increasing, particularly for those under fourteen.[5]

But suicide and euthanasia are not only an offense against human dignity; they also usurp the purpose and plan of God in our lives. "The LORD brings death and makes alive; he brings down to the grave and raises up," says 1 Samuel 2:6. "For every living soul belongs to me," says the Lord, "the father as well as the son—both alike belong to me. The soul who sins is the one who will die" (Ezekiel 18:4).

In committing suicide, perhaps more than in any other act, we defiantly say, "I am the master of my fate. I am the captain of my soul. I do determine my own destiny." It is the ultimate expression of futility. But it is also the ultimate expression of selfishness and rebellion against God.

Now even as you read this you may be thinking, *But what about the man who is terminally ill and in such great pain he can't stand it? What about the woman who is in such deep emotional despair, whose life is so awful that she can't bear living another day? What about people who are so lonely and alienated that they can no longer exist with the deadness inside?*

Surely it saddens us, as men and women of compassion, to see someone in such hopelessness and despair that he or

141

she would rather commit suicide than live another moment. But suicide is not the answer. Our only true relief is found in Christ. He is the One who truly understands our pain and our infirmities, the One who is the answer to our deepest longings, the One who endured death so that we might discover life.

You may also be thinking: *I've sat at the bedside of a loved one whose death was long and painful. A caring physician suggested that as long as we kept the treatments going we were just prolonging the end and preventing the inevitable. We didn't seem to be extending any kind of quality life, let along preserving the sanctity of life, so we withdrew all support and let our loved one pass on.*

Physicians down through the ages have stopped treatments and extraordinary means of keeping someone alive when the end is inevitable. That is what it sometimes takes to allow another human being to die with dignity. Death with dignity is not a euphemism for euthanasia. It is not the same as the so-called mercy killing of a Jack Kevorkian.

As Christians, we must clearly understand that all life, whatever quality it has, belongs to God. He is both the giver and the taker of life. We must not turn our minds and souls over to the Destroyer.

Abortion

If suicide is an epidemic, abortion is a national disgrace on such a scale that the Nazi holocaust pales in statistical comparison. The most recent statistics show that reported abortions are taking place at the rate of 23,286 per week.[6] Imagine each week the major basketball arena in your city being filled to overflowing capacity with an aborted baby in every seat. Unthinkable? Unconscionable? Undeniable!

Unfortunately, much of the abortion debate is not a debate at all; it's a shouting match. It's one group on one side yelling their slogans, and the group on the other side retaliating with their slogans. But is anybody listening? If we are truly going to debate, we need to understand the belief system behind the slogans. If we think we can win by shouting louder, we're sadly deluded.

I was behind a car the other day that carried a bumper sticker that said, "Pro-family, Pro-kids, Pro-choice." Now, that is representative of the muddle-headedness that surrounds the issue. But if I were going to engage this young couple in dialogue with any hope of them hearing me, I would need to shut up long enough to allow them to express their beliefs.

If we are to show others the fallacy of their beliefs, we have to understand what those beliefs are. If they believe that there is no authority over us, that there is no personal, creator God who reigns, that there is no reason for our existence, and that we prolong our lives by chance and die in oblivion, then there is no reason in the world why they should value the life of an unborn child.

At the same time, we must be able to articulate the fact that we are not simply promoting some hollow, knee-jerk crusade. Instead, we are upholding the sixth commandment and the sanctity of human life as the Creator God ordained.

The beginning of life is not a scientific matter; it is a moral matter. Our godless friends are determined to prove—if not in the laboratory, then by law—that a fetus is not a human being because they still cannot quite bring themselves to say that it is all right to murder children. The day may not be far off when they will decide that it is. And on that day, the debate will be over. Because then people will be honest enough to say, "We don't care. We know this fetus is a child, and we don't want a child. And since we are in control of things, we can take that child's life."

But the truth is that the fetus in the womb is, from the moment of conception, a human being in the process of arriving. The fact that for several months that fetus cannot survive outside the womb does not affect its right to the same protection other human beings merit, and which it will itself immediately merit as soon as it slips from the womb.

Some who are reading this may have personally faced the choice of abortion in their own lives. God is as merciful in relation to that sin as He is to all others when we seek salvation and forgiveness through the sacrificial blood of His Son. So don't allow the burden of your own past to keep you from Him. If you have not dealt with your sin, turn to Him now. And if you have already done so, don't allow the devil to rummage around in areas of sin for which you have already been forgiven.

Hidden Homicide

As we think about the forces of evil that are rampant in our culture, we sometimes feel such a rising tide of moral indignation that we wonder how we can bear it a moment longer. We have prayed, voted, marched, picketed, and spoken out. There is no question that we are on the Lord's side on this matter of the sanctity of life. The problem is that we have applied "You shall not kill" to everyone but ourselves.

"But wait just a minute," you say. "I have never killed anyone. And I never would, except in defense of my family or my country." Derek Prime points out that human attitudes and emotions that can give rise to murder are forbidden by this commandment. "At first sight the sixth commandment appears to be concerned with the murderous act alone, but the Lord Jesus gave the commandment a further and deeper meaning; all sins that lead to murder, and are the causes of it, are forbidden."[7]

Jesus knew that many of us would forget that every commandment applies to every one of us, so in the Sermon on the Mount, He made it clear that we need a standard of righteousness that is greater than an outward keeping of the Law. Obedience to God's Law, He said, begins deep in the heart. And so, on the issue of killing, He said, "You have heard that it was said to the people long ago, 'Do not murder, and anyone who murders will be subject to judgment.' But I tell you that anyone who is angry with his brother will be subject to judgment. Again, anyone who says to his brother, 'Raca,' is answerable to the Sanhedrin. But anyone who says, 'You fool!' will be in danger of the fire of hell" (Matthew 5:21–22).

Just because we may not have committed a violent act against anyone, just because we have not physically murdered someone, are we to imagine ourselves to be in the clear?

Ah, but have I hated someone? Have I wished someone harm or evil or misfortune?

Did you ever drive away from a business meeting thinking, "I'd like to kill that guy"? Ever get so frustrated or angry with someone that you called them "a total idiot"—to their face, to others, or just to yourself? That's what "Raca" means: empty head, idiot, fool. And Jesus said that anyone who calls or thinks of his brother or sister as "an empty-headed fool" is subject to the same judgment as those who commit murder.

Just because I haven't shed someone's blood, doesn't mean I'm innocent. My heart and mind have harbored thoughts and feelings that are as foul as murder. We kill people all the time with our contemptuous anger, our animosity and malice, our hostility and gossip. Little hidden murders.

"With the tongue we praise our Lord and Father, and with it we curse men, who have been made in God's likeness. Out of the same mouth come praise and cursing. My brothers, this should not be" (James 3:9–10).

Sin is sin. Abortion kills. So does gossip. Murder is lethal. So is hatred.

The Law says, "No murder." The spirit of the Law says, "You shall not cut down one another in any way." Gossip that disfigures and destroys. Malice that desecrates and diminishes. Anger that criticizes. Hatred that destroys. Little hidden murders.

Sin is sin. When you think about suicide, euthanasia, abortion, and homicide, remember what Jesus taught in Matthew 5:21.

Jesus told the Pharisees that they could keep the letter of the Law all they wanted, but when they turned their critical and vicious tongues on others, they were in danger of hellfire.

TRUTH IS HARD, BUT GRACE IS GOOD

Truth is hard, isn't it? The drive to make ourselves right with God—to prove to Him that we are good enough to deserve His grace and favor—continues long after we have surrendered our lives to Christ. We say we count on His death to save us. We say we count on God's grace and Holy Spirit to work in us and set us apart for His use. But the truth is, our deeply rooted pride says, "I won't be so utterly dependent upon God as to admit there is *nothing* I can do for myself." And then we hear Jesus say, "So you don't murder. That's fine. But do you ever fail to see someone else as the Father sees them—in need of His love and mercy? Do you see them though the eyes of evil judgment—as deserving of hell? Then in your heart you are a killer."

What do we do with these hearts of ours? We need to guard them and when we lie on our beds at the end of the day, often reflecting on how we've been treated by others, we need to make sure that we don't fall asleep angry and by doing so give the devil a foothold. Before we became Christians it was customary for us to tolerate, even cultivate bitterness, anger, brawling, slander, and malice but that belongs to the "old days" and by the Spirit's help must be put away. In its place should be the kind of self-sacrificing love that seeks to protect and preserve our neighbors.

We must discover God's way out of our predicament. We must give up on the idea that by working hard to keep His commands we may make ourselves acceptable to Him and achieve a right standing before Him. After looking closely at just six of His commandments, it should be clear to us that we can't.

Although we fail, although we will never conform to the Law perfectly in heart and mind and action, the new life God has secured for us in Christ enables us to be transformed. And the ministry of the Holy Spirit in our lives enables us to be conformed to the will of God. Then, as the Holy Spirit works in our hearts, we find pleasure in God Himself, and thus we both delight in Him and are empowered from within to obey His commands.

Remember, the Law is not a ladder up which we climb to forgiveness. It is a mirror in which we see ourselves in need of a Savior and in need of the power of the Holy Spirit to clothe us in His righteousness.

Postscript

The Bible acknowledges three exceptions in the taking of human life that do not violate this commandment. One is the crime of manslaughter. In the Old Testament the cities of refuge provided a safe haven for those guilty of manslaughter so that the circumstances, which resulted in the loss of life, could be reviewed and the case properly tried. For example if someone had taken the life of a person in self-defense, this was not treated as murder. We distinguish today in our courts between the loss of life that has taken place in a tragic traffic accident (manslaughter) and the willful destruction of life in a premeditated act of violence.

Another is the lawfulness of defensive war. The concept of a "just war" is cause for real discussion but it is clear from Scripture that the taking of life in the time of war is not regarded as murder.

The third area is the exercise of capital punishment. Since this is an area of intense debate, I will address it at greater length.

In Romans 13 Paul establishes the fact that God has ordained the institution of civil government. Because it has a divine sanction, those who govern may exercise authority and those who are governed submit to it.

In the previous chapter Paul instructs the believers not to take revenge. In the opening verse of chapter 13 he points out that what we, as individuals must not do, the government has been charged with doing—exercising on God's behalf, vengeance on those who practice evil.

What Paul is establishing is this: All human authority is derived from God's authority. So for example, as we saw in the last commandment, we obey our parents who are put in position by God's perfect design. When Jesus was before Pilate, He said to him: "You would have no power [authority] over me if it were not given to you from above" (John 19:11). Commenting on this, John Stott says, "Pilate misused his authority to condemn Jesus, nevertheless, the authority he used to do this had been delegated to him by God."[8]

Peter tells his readers that the restraint and punishment of evil is the state's responsibility. Government has been instituted by God, "to punish those who do wrong and to commend those who do right" (1 Peter 2:14).

The death penalty affirms the unique value of human life. "Whoever sheds the blood of man, by man shall his blood be shed; for in the image of God has God made man." That verse in Genesis 9:6 is another reminder of the way in which our view of the world affects our philosophical and moral decisions. There is a huge difference between the view that sees man as just a random collection of molecules and the view which regards man as being the unique creation of a personal creator to whom he is accountable. The Bible assigns special value to the life of man because he has been created in the image of God. Here is man's dignity. He is a moral agent responsible for his actions. To view him as a patient to be manipulated for the good of society is, as C. S. Lewis wrote, to strip him of his dignity. "To be punished however severely, because we have deserved it, because we ought to have known better is to be treated as a human person made in God's image."[9]

The church has a responsibility when the civil magistrate fails to exercise his God-given authority to "wield the sword," to urge the state to exercise capital punishment and in doing so to uphold the sanctity of human life.

Since life is God's gift and is on loan to us by God it is protected by the sixth commandment.

Each of us has been created with an innate sense of right and wrong. We know that crime should be punished. We recognize that the punishment should fit the crime. We also know, if we are honest, that death is the appropriate punishment for the highest of all crimes—murder. That this is the instinctive judgment of men and women is clearly seen by our desire to take judgment into our own hands. Where the regular, lawful infliction of death as a judicial penalty is abolished, it will tend to be inflicted by the avenger. The story of the Wild West is in part the record of a developing society choosing either the exercise of fair trials by constituted authorities or the giving of itself to the blind spirit of revenge.

Charles Hodge writes: "Experience teaches that where human life is undervalued it is insecure; that where the murderer escapes with impunity or is inadequately punished, homicides are fearfully multiplied. The practical question, therefore is, Who is to die? The innocent man or the murderer?"

We have said enough to leave us in no doubt that this is a difficult issue. Many oppose capital punishment on the grounds that it is too easy to make a mistake and execute the wrong person. Certainly the utmost care needs to be taken in this regard, but the fallibility of the system does not negate the necessity of the sentence.

This is also an issue that is surrounded by confused thinking and passionate convictions. At the heart of the debate is the assertion that the death penalty is to be equated with capital murder because both actions end in the taking of human life. So they are regarded as morally equivalent. At its most extreme we find the death penalty equated with the Nazi holocaust. Is it not possible to see a moral distinction between the slaughter of twelve million totally innocent men, women, and children and the just execution of a cold, rage-twisted twenty-eight-year-old who delivered death to 168 men, women and children with a one-ton bomb on wheels? Remember Timothy McVeigh?

I am grateful for this insight:

- The idea that if two acts have the same result they are morally equivalent is an untenable position.
- Is the repossession of property in payment of a debt the same as auto theft?
- Are kidnapping and imprisonment the same since both involve being retained against one's will?
- Is killing in self-defense the same as capital murder since both end in taking life?

At the very core of the discussion is the matter of God's sovereign right to rule. To suggest that the sixth commandment forbids capital punishment is to set God against Himself. Capital punishment should not be seen as being inflicted to gratify revenge but in order to serve justice and to preserve the sanctity of life and the well-being of human society.

YOU SHALL NOT COMMIT ADULTERY

You shall not commit adultery.

—EXODUS 20:14

In 1631, the printers of one edition of the King James Bible were fined £300 pounds by Archbishop Laud—the equivalent of a lifetime's earnings. Their crime consisted in leaving one word out of the biblical text. By omitting the word *not,* they had turned the seventh commandment on its head. And so it read: "You shall commit adultery." As a result, this 1631 edition became known as "the wicked Bible." It is hard to imagine a similar reaction today in light of the massive landslide in private and public morality.

In 2003 adultery is generally regarded as a private activity between consenting adults with little public consequence. It was not always so. In 1963 when Richard Burton and Elizabeth Taylor began an affair during the filming of *Cleopatra,* they were shunned and Taylor was condemned even in Hollywood for stealing Burton from his wife. In 1987, Gary Hart withdrew from the Democratic primary because of his relationship with Donna Rice. How vastly different from the self-serving, unrepentant bravado that marked the Clinton era. Fifty years earlier in Great Britain, Lord Justice Denning had seen the writing on the wall, pointing out that adultery, or infidelity was no longer regarded as a barrier on the road to government service, whereas any other form of stealing would have meant the end of a career.

Long ago and far away, a young Israelite set the standard for all who are tempted to commit adultery when he responded to the seductive advances of his boss's wife by declaring: "How then could I do such a wicked thing and sin against God?" (Genesis 39:9). I recently listened to a very straightforward sermon on this commandment. The preacher pulled no punches in providing a picture of the physical, emotional, and spiritual carnage that results from breaking this commandment. In doing so he (I think unwittingly) failed to point out the fact that to commit adultery is not just to offend another human being; it is to sin against God because it offends His Law. Joseph didn't reason with himself or his seductress along the lines of "We might get caught," or "We will be hurt by this," or any other pragmatic consideration. Sexual sin, as with every other sin, is a wicked thing against God. We fail to acknowledge this to our peril. We will return to this, but first we should consider the positive side of the command.

The Shorter Catechism's answer to what is required in the seventh commandment is this: "The seventh commandment requires the preservation of our own and our neighbor's chastity, in heart, speech, and behavior." In short, it teaches the sanctity of marriage. Marriage is not an accidental but a purposeful, essential element of creation. It is a divine institution providing the cornerstone of civil society. It is, if you like, quite simply, God's idea.

It is not a convention to be adopted as a humanly devised experiment. Nor is it a consequence to be absorbed. It is quite common today for couples to reverse God's order of things by putting sex before marriage and then often reluctantly formalizing their mating habits in a marriage ceremony. It certainly is not as a journalist in Britain in the seventies suggested, a cage to be avoided. The feminist essayist and columnist Jill Tweedie wrote in *The Guardian:* "The pundits blame the rising divorce rate on our godlessness, our selfishness, our lustfulness. I blame it on the wrongful expectation of thinking that people can live together as long as they both shall live. I think this expectation goes against our deepest nature, stunting our growth and requiring us to distort our lives to fulfill it. Outside the bonds of Christian marriage we will, I hope, learn for the first time what love is all about."[1]

On this side of the Atlantic and around the same time, the sociologist Morton Hunt was touting polygamy as being better suited to the emotional capacities and requirements of many people, particularly men: "It offers them renewed excitement and continual expressions of personal rediscovery. It is an answer to the boredom of lifelong monogamy."

This kind of thinking is far more prevalent in our culture than we may be prepared to admit. The wholesale rejection of the seventh commandment ought to be a matter of shame; instead, it feeds the insatiable appetite of a society that on the one hand bemoans the breakdown of the family and on the other hand excuses infidelity and adultery. In the movie *The Graduate,* an affair was viewed as just "little secret" to be hidden from the kids. Hiding it from the children is, of course, just not possible. Acute emotional damage is an almost inevitable result of the violation of God's command.

The marriage ceremony reminds us that the welfare of

human society hinges upon the marriage bond being held in honor. Marriage is what the theologians refer to as a *Creation ordinance.* "God created man in his own image, in the image of God he created him; male and female he created them" (Genesis 1:27). Whether the debate is about marriage or abortion, the death penalty, euthanasia, or other moral and philosophical questions, the watershed issue is Creation. Is man simply a random collection of molecules, the result of time plus matter plus chance? Or is he the unique creation of a personal God who has stamped him with His image and made him for a relationship with Himself? This is not the occasion to tease out the implications of these two diametrically opposed views. The underlying conviction with which I come to these commands is that it is only when we recognize ourselves to be, in distinction from the animals, the most special and greatest work of God that we can live a truly human life.

In the verse we have just quoted there is a quick change from "him" to "them." Man is defined as "male and female," the two components of a single entity. The opening verses of Genesis 5 reinforce this: "When God created man, he made him in the likeness of God. He created them male and female and blessed them. And when they were created, he called them 'man.'"

"They are Mr. and Mrs. Adam . . . because, in their oneness, they are the essential components of that unique entity in creation, 'man in the image of God.'"[2] The same writer points out that the Creator brings the female into being by making the male incomplete (Genesis 2:22) and then finds completion in receiving back what was taken from him. In the same way, the female is "built" in separation from her true origin, and it is in union with the male that she returns to where and what she should be; if you like, she "comes home." There is a mystery in this to which Paul refers in Ephesians 5:31–32.

George Orwell said that a restatement of the obvious is sometimes the first duty of a responsible man. It is therefore worth restating what was once obvious and commonly held: *Marriage involves a man and a woman.* From the very creation of mankind and the foundation of civil order, God intended marriage to be an inseparable union between husband and wife. In that context only is it possible to make sense of the biblical injunction: "Be fruitful and increase in number; fill the earth and subdue it" (Genesis 1:28). The most obvious argument against the lesbian and homosexual agenda is human physiology! A light bulb needs a socket if there is to be illumination. Two sockets on their own are incapable of light, and the same is true for two bulbs. Homosexuality in practice involves a perverted use of the human body, and it is a forsaking of the natural for the unnatural. It is not a marriage. It cannot be.

Marriage, the Bible says, is a loving, lasting, binding, solemn, exclusive covenant of companionship in which a man and a woman begin to think, act, and feel as one. The focus for husband and wife is to be upon pleasing one another. To become "one flesh" means that to hurt one's partner is to hurt oneself. The pattern for each is clear. The husband is to love his wife sacrificially, protecting and cherishing her; and the wife is to love, honor, and obey her husband. Far from being a cage, as Tweedie suggested, this is the pathway to freedom. Freedom to live without the daily threat of disease or divorce or the disruptive impact of lustful preoccupations. In the privacy and sanctity of marriage there is comfort and safety. When Solomon warned his son about the honey-lipped advances of the adulteress, he then described marriage in the most attractive terms.

Drink water from your own cistern,
    running water from your own well.
Should your springs overflow in the streets,
    your streams of water in public squares?
Let them be yours alone,
    never to be shared with strangers.
May your fountain be blessed,
    and may you rejoice in the wife of your youth.
A loving doe, a graceful deer—
    may her breasts satisfy you always,
    may you ever be captivated by her love.
Why be captivated, my son, by an adulteress?
    Why embrace the bosom of another man's wife?
        —PROVERBS 5:15–20

Faithfulness in marriage is vital to its well-being. In the marriage ceremony, the couple are calling upon God and the congregation to bear witness to the vows they are making to each other. They do so in the awareness that the commitment they are making is "until death us do part." Over the years, I have learned to steer couples away from their often well-intentioned desire to write their own vows. More often than not they prove to be expressions of their feelings rather than promises to be kept. It is essential that the couple understand that they are entering into a covenant before God in which they agree to do or refrain from doing certain acts. They commit themselves to each other for life and on the basis of their solemn vows they become one.

The prophet calls upon the men of his generation: "So guard yourself in your spirit, and do not break faith with the wife of your youth" (Malachi 2:15). We need to appoint moral sentries to guard our hearts, because losing the battle there is often the first step on the road to disaster. As a boy I was reminded frequently of the fact that we reap what we sow. My own parents taught me the importance of this by pointing out how our choices in the "small things" affect the "big things" later on. They encouraged me to memorize these lines:

Sow a thought, reap an action.

Sow an action, reap a habit.

Sow a habit, reap a character.

Sow a character, reap a destiny.

This fits with what the Bible clearly teaches.

The Shorter Catechism asks not only what is *required* by the seventh commandment but also what is *forbidden* by it. The seventh commandment forbids all unchaste thoughts, words, and actions. To commit adultery is to sin against God, our body, the partner in the affair, our spouse, and our partner's spouse. Adultery is a betrayal, an intrusion, and a rejection of God's instruction, which has been provided for our good. The adulterer separates what God has joined together and fails to love his neighbor as himself.

God ordained marriage and He presides over marriages and desires that the marriage bed be kept pure. He assures us that He will judge the adulterer and all the sexually immoral, to fill us with fear and to keep us from sin. Therefore, says Calvin, "When we hear the word *adultery* it ought to be detestable to us, as if men deliberately wanted to despise God, and like raging beasts wanted to break the sacred bond that he has established in marriage."[3]

We must be diligent in seeing that we do not set aside God's command by becoming flippant in our use of language, using words in a manner that trivializes what God detests. Obscenity, foolish talk, and course joking too easily pave the way to sexual immorality. We are familiar with the notion of "talking ourselves or others into something." It is imperative that we take seriously Paul's injunction, "Do not let any unwholesome talk come out of your mouths" (Ephesians 4:29).

But even if we have managed to gain mastery over our bodies and our speech, we dare not rest content in the assumption that we have thereby obeyed the seventh commandment. God is not merely concerned to forbid the act of adultery but also to forbid the indulgence of evil affections. What a hammer blow to the Pharisees in Jesus' day when He confronted them with the adultery of the heart: "You have heard that it was said, 'Do not commit adultery.' But I tell you that anyone who looks at a woman lustfully has already committed adultery with her in his heart" (Matthew 5:27–28).

When a man looks upon another man's wife with lust, he is an adulterer in God's eyes. A wife must not surrender herself to lascivious thoughts when she thinks about a married man, for to do so is to be guilty of adultery in her heart. If we are to maintain purity of heart and to glorify God with our bodies, we must seek to avoid those occasions that lead us into immorality. This is to take seriously Solomon's word to his son: "Above all else, guard your heart, for it is the wellspring of life. Put away perversity from your mouth; keep corrupt talk far from your lips. Let your eyes look straight ahead, fix your gaze directly before you" (Proverbs 4:23–25).

Derek Prime has cautioned us not to allow our hearts to follow our eyes. Such counsel is intensely practical and vitally necessary when we consider how thoughts, words, and deeds may become the occasion of sin. For this very reason

Job declared, "I made a covenant with my eyes not to look lustfully at a girl" (Job 31:1).

The Heidelberg Catechism has a more comprehensive answer than is provided by the Shorter Catechism to the question, "What does the seventh commandment teach?" "God forbids all unchaste actions, gestures, words, thoughts, desires and whatever may excite another person to them." Calvin preached on this commandment to his congregation in Geneva on July 2, 1555. By way of application he pointed out that if they would take seriously what the Bible had to say about these issues, then

> *we would no longer see lewdness in dress, or in gestures, or in speech, as the world currently provides too excessive a license. For when men and women dress in such a way as to seduce each other and to entice each other into adultery, are they not all the more engaged in prostitution? It is true that they argue: "Oh, I haven't committed adultery." But in doing so they only reveal that they are a prey to Satan and would like to trap others as much as possible. Consequently, they are like a type of adulterer in God's sight, as all licentiousness and excessiveness in dress is only asking to be engulfed by the snares.*

One can only begin to imagine what Calvin would have to say about how easily lust may be stirred by the dress code of contemporary fashion. In passing, we might note that girls have a particular responsibility in this. Whatever the style they choose, it is important that they recognize the difference between making themselves attractive and making themselves deliberately seductive. Girls know the difference, and so do boys!

While it is true that to the pure all things are pure, we must remain alert to the ways in which the Evil One can trip us up. The hymn writer encourages us to learn to "tremble at the very approach of sin." So grave is this matter that Jesus employed chilling metaphors (gouging out eyes, cutting off hands) to call for the most ruthless action to be taken to ensure that the offender is not thrown into hell (Matthew 5:21–30).

This may be the appropriate moment to address a perverse form of thinking I have encountered over the years. The person reasons as follows: *Since I have already committed adultery in my heart, I might as well go ahead and follow through with the action; either way I am guilty.* This is based on the assumption that there is no difference between mental and physical adultery. Without lessening the impact of Jesus' teaching, we need to recognize that there are substantial differences between daydreaming lust and sexual intercourse/adultery.

- Adultery breaks the marriage covenant; adulterous thoughts do not.
- Adultery provides the grounds for divorce; mental adultery does not.
- Adultery violates and defiles each other's bodies; its mental counterpart does not.
- Adultery is the vehicle for sexually transmitted diseases; whereas the mind is not.

Instead of allowing lust to conceive and give birth to further sin, we need to get rid of *all* moral filth and the evil that is so prevalent and humbly accept the Word of God in its warnings and corrections and ask God by His Spirit to purify our heart. Calvin says:

If you aspire to obedience, let neither your heart burn with wicked lust within, nor your eyes wantonly run into corrupt

desires, nor your body be decked with bawdy ornaments, nor
your tongue seduce your mind to like thoughts with filthy
words, nor your appetite inflame it with intemperance. For all
vices of this sort are like blemishes, which besmirch the purity
of chastity." (Institutes, 408)

"DANGER! KEEP OUT!"

Only a fool climbs the fence that bears this warning. It is posted to protect us from injury and physical harm. In the same way, the Bible warns against danger in the moral and spiritual realm. The most vulnerable individuals are those who see the warning as important for everyone but themselves. The following fiction is sadly too easy to write. This story has been repeated too many times in the past twenty-eight years of pastoral ministry.

"We are just good friends," Jack sought to reassure himself with the thought. "Thelma is a good business associate, that's all. I respect her for her ability. There's nothing wrong with that." Maybe not, but some eight months later it was Thelma, and not his wife, who was waking up beside Jack. Two marriages were destroyed.

How did this happen? Were Jack and Thelma moral reprobates? Not at all. They started out, in fact, a lot like many others—responsible Christian people with no thought or intention of ever cheating on their spouses.

Does it sound a little far-fetched? Be careful—that's what Jack and Thelma were thinking when their casual encounters began to increase in length and frequency. They were so sure of themselves that neither saw the need to put up hedges to protect against an affair developing. It all started innocently enough; but then slowly, imperceptibly, they began to depend on each other emotionally. They shared private plans and ambitions, justified lunches together, and exchanged physical touches, which they deemed fraternal and platonic. They liked each other, became special to each other, became infatuated with each other, and instead of running for their lives, they led each other as lambs to the slaughter.

The Law of God provides a boundary, a fence for our protection, a pathway to safety and freedom. To wander from it is to flirt with danger. In terms of the story above, we dare not accept as normal the lingering attraction, the casual flirtation, the fleeting fantasy. Almost inevitably we will find ourselves in the wrong place at the wrong time. Truth is not only stranger than fiction; it is more compelling by way of illustration. A few years ago a very gifted and prominent pastor in the U.K. left his wife and family in favor of a friend. Among the many articles which followed this disclosure was one in the London *Daily Telegraph,* written by Ann Atkins. She mentioned how she could hardly think of anyone less likely to abandon his loved ones, but she said she was not surprised; she was prepared for a far more important reason.

> *When I was younger, I used to find some Christian teaching rather gloomy. The doctrine of total depravity, for instance. I preferred to think everyone's jolly nice, really. And so we are: we are made in the image of God with the divine stamp on us all. But the Bible also teaches that we have fallen from this created ideal and now are rotten through and through—all of us. I have friends who consider this deeply offensive. But as I have got older, I have found it increasingly liberating.*
>
> *You see, I, too, am an adulterer. A few years ago, I was in a remote part of the world, alone with the owner of an idyllic island. As the days went by he became more attentive and more attractive. It was an extremely pleasant sensation. I was*

enjoying myself greatly, my work required me to be there, and my head insisted that I was above temptation. But I am not. The Bible tells me so. Consequently, I knew I must leave urgently. I did. By the grace of God, I didn't commit adultery. Not then. And not yet. But it's there, in my heart, biding its time. Jesus said that makes me as bad as the worst offender. Happily, because I've always been taught that I am capable of adultery, I have always been on my guard against it. After all, it doesn't start when you jump into bed with your lover—but months, years earlier, when you tell yourself that your friend understands you better than your spouse.

Run for Your Life!

We return to the story of Joseph as a helpful example of someone who faced the temptation to adultery head-on and did not give in.

Potipher's wife had allowed her heart to follow her eyes. She was infatuated with the handsome Hebrew slave. Her proposition was straightforward and sustained. When she finally got her hands on Joseph, his only recourse was to flee. How did he do it? He responded by asking the question, "What is the right thing to do?" And he knew the answer. To violate the marriage bed of Potiphar and his wife would be to sin against God. He said no to temptation, and he ratified his decision on a daily basis by not only refusing her advances but by refusing even to be in her company. He understood that it can take thirty years to build a character and only five minutes to ruin it, and so when push came to shove, he determined it would be better to lose his cloak than his character. So he ran for his life.

In seeking to learn from his example and to follow it, we will be helped by taking several steps.

Practicing the Presence of God

We need to remind ourselves that our heavenly Father knows when we sit down and when we stand and our words before we speak. We will soon stand before Him in judgment, and we should never consider doing anything that we would not do if we knew it to be the last hour of our lives.

Memorizing the Word of God

We should keep the Word of God in our hearts so that our walk might be true. Psalm 119 says, "How can a young man keep his way pure? By living according to your word. . . . I have hidden your word in my heart that I might not sin against you" (vv. 9, 11).

Joining with the People of God

There is safety in numbers. When we isolate ourselves from the company of God's people, we are increasingly vulnerable. The writer to the Hebrews urged them not to give up meeting together as had become the practice of some. Instead, they were to encourage each other and especially as they thought about their final destination (Hebrews 10:25).

God has promised that He will not let us be tempted beyond our ability to bear it. He will provide for us a way of escape (1 Corinthians 10:13). In this confidence we must learn to deal with temptation immediately, realistically, ruthlessly, and consistently. Remember Joseph!

Be Encouraged!

I should imagine that each of us has found reading this chapter an uncomfortable exercise. Hidden thoughts and attitudes of the heart have been brought out into the light and exposed for the sin they are. The Law has proved to be a mirror, and the sight of our reflection saddens us. Some may have been toying with sin, playing mind games, and now you are convicted and convinced that action needs to be taken. Then follow through!

Turn away from everything you know to be wrong in word, thought, and action. Be intensely practical and realistic. Lose the phone number, ditch your computer, cancel the magazine subscription, change your job, alter your daily routine. In short, do whatever it takes to separate yourself from the occasion of sin. Do not look for ways to excuse or justify your conduct. Come to God like the wayward son to his father. Make his words your own, "I have sinned against heaven and against you." The promise of the Bible is that God is faithful and just and will forgive our sins and cleanse our consciences from acts that lead to death so that we might live to serve Him (1 John 1:9). Do you see how the Law also serves as a pedagogue leading us to Christ (Galatians 3:24)? It is only at the cross we see sin punished and mercy made freely available.

Here is hope for the person who has moved beyond the possibility. Having committed adultery, you may feel that you have sinned yourself outside the love of God. Listen! Even adultery, as wrong and terrible as it is, is not the unforgivable sin. You are not trapped fatalistically in the clutches of sin. God's kindness points you to the door marked *Repentance*. To enter is to acknowledge that you are a sinner, that sin is an offence against God and an offence to God. It is to face the fact that God has a legitimate right to exercise judgment and that you are without excuse. The only basis upon which we may appeal is on account of His mercy, His unfailing love, and His great compassion (Psalm 51). And where is all this grace to be found? In the Lord Jesus, who by His death silenced the Law's condemnation by paying the wage it demanded and thus clearing the repentant sinner of all debt. H. G. Spafford exulted in this thought when he wrote:

My sin, oh, the bliss of this glorious thought,

My sin, not in part but the whole,

Is nailed to the cross and I bear it no more

Bless the Lord, Bless the Lord, oh my soul!

So the Law serves as a mirror showing me my condition. It takes me by the hand and leads me to Christ. And then, as Alec Motyer puts it, "The law released from its ceaseless obligation to condemn, is free in Christ to become the means of grace it was also intended to be . . . for in Christ the Law becomes a minister of life to those who set their feet in its paths. The prohibitory 'You shall *not* . . .' becomes the promissory 'You *shall* not.'"[4]

This reminds us of what we learned in the introduction. We are "not under law" as a way of *justification,* and yet we are "under law" as the God-given *pattern of life.* On the pathway to freedom, the travelers may be heard saying to each other, "We know that we have come to know Him because we keep His commands."

POSTSCRIPT

Although we did not address the issue of divorce in the course of this chapter, it is clearly relevant to the discussion. The apparent ease with which professing Christians opt for divorce as a "justifiable" solution to a difficult marriage ought to be a cause for great alarm. It fails to treat seriously what the Bible has to say:

Divorce is something that God hates and marriage should not be entered upon lightly or carelessly seeing divorce as an escape route (Malachi 2:16; Matthew 19:9).

The covenant of marriage is binding, lifelong, and cannot be set aside at the will of either of the parties; it is only properly dissolved by the death of one of the partners (Matthew 19:3–9).

A husband who divorces his wife, except for marital unfaithfulness, and marries another, commits adultery (Matthew 19:9; Mark 10:1–12).

A wife is an adulteress if, apart from the same exception, she marries another man while her husband is still alive (Romans 7:3).

Marital unfaithfulness may be, but need not be, grounds for divorce. The reason being that the unique one-flesh reality in marriage has been rent by the monstrosity of sexual intercourse with someone other than one's spouse (Matthew 19:9).

If either the husband or wife as the offended party should divorce their partner on the grounds of marital unfaithfulness and then marry someone else, they commit no offense (Matthew 5:32; Mark 10:11–12).

"Marriage should be honored by all, and the marriage bed kept pure, for God will judge the adulterer and all the sexually immoral" (Hebrews 13:4).

8

I WAS ONLY BORROWING IT

You shall not steal.

—EXODUS 20:15

$\mathcal{N}$ext Sunday maybe you should preach on Exodus 20:15." This entry in our visitor's book for the nineteenth of June 1978 is certainly one of the more intriguing comments to appear beside the names of our overnight guests. David and Margie were visiting us in Scotland. They were en route to Africa where they were to be married. Given that they were both children of missionary parents, it seemed appropriate to introduce them to the nearby birthplace of Dr. David Livingstone, the legendary missionary to Africa. While they were exploring the museum, a thief decided to explore their car. The window of their car was smashed with a brick and their possessions, including Margie's wedding dress, were stolen. The police would later find the dress discarded in a ditch, but everything else was gone forever. Sadly our young friends' experience is not unique.

The unlawful taking of possessions belonging to another

in such crimes as shoplifting, pocket picking, purse snatching, and theft of motor vehicles and bicycles takes place routinely in our society. According to one report, larceny/ theft makes up 56 percent of all the crime committed in America. A four-year college student has a 53 percent chance of having his or her bike stolen. Apparently the crime of bicycle theft is at epidemic proportions! Bicycle theft is a billion-dollar-a-year business in the United States, with an estimated five and one half million bicycles stolen each year. According to the 2001 *National Retail Security Survey*, U.S. retailers lost more than $13.2 billion from employee theft. Of the $29 billion in losses reported last year by retailers, employee theft made up a larger percentage (44.5%) than shoplifting (32.7%).[1] Employee theft and shoplifting together account for the largest source of property crime committed annually in the United States. This massive loss of proper respect for other people's property presents yet another example of the way in which the moral fabric of our society is unraveling.

I recently read of a school teacher who, in seeking to impress upon her class the importance of honesty, confronted them with this question: "Suppose you found a briefcase with half a million dollars in it. What would you do?" One boy immediately replied, "If it belonged to a poor family, I'd return it. But if it belonged to a rich person, I'd keep it."

And so it seems that Robin Hood is as much a hero today as he was in Sherwood Forest. The Robin Hood principle, or lack of principle, is trotted out in defense of theft. The relativism that is so pervasive in our culture extends to the matter of personal property. A person may reason as follows: "I do not feel right about taking money from my sister's wallet, but I don't think it is wrong to steal from an institution. After all, they have so much money they'll never miss it. They can afford it, and I'm not hurting anyone."

In his novel *Oliver Twist,* Charles Dickens created a character known as the "Artful Dodger." He was, among other things, a master pickpocket and expert at dodging the London Bobbies who were constantly on his trail. Judging from the statistics just quoted, it would seem legitimate to suggest that we are becoming a society of dodgers. Men and women are increasingly adept at building rationales for taking what is not theirs, dodging God's eighth commandment with their twisted logic.

But God does not accept any human rationale for dishonest dealings. Every line of reasoning that aims to nullify God's Law is a string of lies based on the greater lie: That human beings can with impunity ignore God's Law and shift reality around whenever it suits their wants and needs. By means of this straightforward command, "You shall not steal," God, says Calvin, motivates us to hate all fraud, all wrong, and all extortion that can possibly be done against another's property. The Christian needs to be unwavering and unashamed in saying no to theft and yes to honest endeavor. Paul reminds his readers in Ephesus of the fact that they have been, "created to be like God in true righteousness and holiness." And one of the marks of their new life is in this: "He who has been stealing must steal no longer, but must work, doing something useful with his own hands, that he may have something to share with those in need" (Ephesians 4:28).

The intense practicality is difficult to miss! The Bible speaks so clearly to the matters that concern us most. There is hardly a magazine cover in the grocery store checkout that does not tackle the issues of human relationships, the family in particular, and of course sex and money. Each of these subjects is covered in these commandments, which mark out for us freedom's pathway. When we consider the importance of honest hard work and the need to respect the property of others, we are dealing with what is a generally agreed-upon standard. It is unnecessary to read thick tomes in order to learn that stealing is wrong. Men and women "know" that they should not seek to become rich at the expense of their neighbors and that they should not invade the rights of others by walking off with their bicycle or any part of property that does not belong to them. The very fact that men and women are aware of the legitimacy of this command is evidence of their having been made in God's image with a sense of right and wrong. When we turn to the Bible, we find it explains *why* it is wrong to steal. Two principles stand behind the "do not steal" injunction.

1. God Establishes the Individual's Right to Private Property.

By implication this commandment teaches the legitimacy and dignity of possessions lawfully acquired and properly enjoyed. David declares: "Yours, O LORD, is the kingdom; you are exalted as head over all. Wealth and honor come from you; you are the ruler of all things" (1 Chronicles 29:11–12). Any attempt to deny or to diminish the significance of private, personal ownership fails to recognize that God has put us together in such a way that part of our human dignity is wrapped up in our desire for and need of this right of exclusive possession. As Derek Prime puts it, "The foundation of the right of property is God's will."[2]

As a young man growing up in the sixties with the emphasis on communal lifestyle, I was forced to examine the Scriptures carefully so as not to be unduly influenced by some who were teaching a form of communized Christianity.

I came to see that what was *described* as taking place in Jerusalem after Pentecost was not *prescribed* for God's people. I learned that the sudden demise of Ananias and Sapphira was not on account of their private ownership but because of their deceitfulness in pretending to give all the proceeds when they were in fact keeping back some. The Bible does not forbid the right of private ownership; it establishes it. And whether money or possessions become ours as a result of inheritance, or a gift, or honest endeavor, we learn from the words of James, that "every good and perfect gift is from above, coming down from the Father" (James 1:17).

It is God who grants to us the ability to get wealth and accumulate worldly goods. Consequently when we invade another's property and steal from them, we sin against God. The same David who articulated so clearly the source of private property realized to his great shame that in taking what did not belong to him he had not only harmed others but had sinned against God. He stole from Bathsheba her purity, her reputation, and her husband's life. "Against you, you only, have I sinned and done what is evil in your sight" (Psalm 51:4).

We do well to notice here how difficult it is to break just one commandment. One sin leads inevitably to another. David broke the first commandment by putting himself before God. He broke the tenth by coveting another man's wife. He broke the ninth in hatching the plot. He broke the eighth in stealing what wasn't his to take. He broke the seventh in committing adultery and the sixth in arranging for Uriah to be killed. Once again, we see how important it is that in our preaching and teaching we are declaring the righteous standard of God's Law. In doing so, the Spirit of God employs it to convict of sin and show to men and women that, although they might have a fairly good view of themselves, in God's sight, they are lawbreakers who deserve only God's judgment.

2. The Individual's Right to Private Property Is Not Absolute.

When God placed Adam in the garden, He gave him stewardship of the rest of His creation. The garden belonged to God and Adam was, if you like, a trustee. The psalmist reminds us that "the earth is the LORD's, and everything in it, the world, and all who live in it" (Psalm 24:1). All the silver and gold, every animal in the forest, and the cattle on a thousand hills belong to the Lord Almighty (Psalm 50:9–12). Man is distinct from the rest of creation, having been made in God's image, and his maker has given him the privilege of exercising stewardship over "the owner's estate." This determines how we view the whole process of the acquiring and disposing of goods. The Christian view of economic theory comes first from an understanding of these principles. Skip Ryan puts it this way: "In capitalism, the money is yours to do with it what you want. In socialism, it belongs to the state, and the state uses it for what the community needs. In Christianity, it's God's, and it must be used as He directs."[3]

Failure to act in this way is a violation of this commandment. Calvin begins his commentary on this command by pointing out that "the purpose of this commandment is: since injustice is an abomination to God, we should render to each man what belongs to him" (*Institutes*, 408). We are not to steal because it offends a holy God, it disregards His Law, and it devalues our neighbor, whose possessions belong to him not by chance but by God's provision.

Once again we realize the importance of the preamble to the Ten Commandments. "I am the LORD your God" (Exodus 20:2). Because God exists and has created man to glorify and enjoy Him, He possesses the right, in and of Himself, to call us to obedience to His Law. If God did not exist, there would be no basis for these laws apart from social convenience. As Dostoevsky put it: "If God is dead, then all things are permissible." From this perspective, stealing might be regarded as not being in the public's best interest, but it would never be regarded as wrong. As Christians we seek to uphold the eighth commandment, not because of the pragmatic benefit of doing so but because these Moral Laws come from God. We do not hold God's Laws to be true because they work, but we affirm that they work because they are true.

There is no doubt that this is clearly an uphill battle, but despite the opposition we face, we seek to live and teach, as Abraham Kuyper put it in his lectures on Calvinism, "*in order that* God's holy ordinances shall be established again in the home, in the school and in the state for the good of the people; to carve as it were into the conscience of the nation the ordinances of the Lord, to which Bible and creation bear witness."[4]

Part of our calling as Christians is to help our secular friends and neighbors to see that these moral norms are not arbitrary or irrational; rather, they are objective and true and they reflect the character of their author, who is a just and holy God.

Perhaps by this point we may feel it is time to move on to the ninth command. After all, if we have not been guilty of "breaking and entry," and we have not stolen by force and "unrestrained brigandage," as Calvin quaintly put it, can't we then safely assume that we have not broken this commandment? But that would be to miss the variety of *ways* in which we can steal and the many *objects* we can steal: not only money and possessions but also time, and as we saw with Bathsheba, even a person's reputation, and the different *subjects* from whom we can steal. We can steal from God and from others and even from ourselves.

Question 110 in the Heidelberg Catechism asks: "What does God forbid in the eighth commandment?" It answers as follows: "He forbids not only outright theft and robbery, punishable by law. But in God's sight theft also includes cheating and swindling our neighbor by schemes made to appear legitimate, such as: Inaccurate measurements of weight, size or volume; fraudulent merchandising; counterfeit money; excessive interest; or any other means forbidden by God. In addition He forbids all greed and pointless squandering of His gifts."

WILL A MAN ROB GOD?

God Himself poses this question to His people. They were blind to the way in which they were guilty of stealing from Him. And so God points out where it is that they have gone wrong. Instead of giving the tithe that was required by the Law, they were fudging the issue, and their selfishness prevented them from discovering all the blessings of heaven which God was prepared to grant them. In a similar fashion, when we fail to recognize the fact that God is Lord of our finances and that all our resources are essentially on loan from Him, we will fail to honor Him in these money matters and thus be guilty of stealing from Him. When we use our breath to magnify ourselves rather than giving Him the glory that He alone deserves, we steal from Him. When we fail to offer our bodies as living sacrifices and spend our time in personal self-indulgence, we steal from Him.

Some years ago I recall hearing about an individual who wished to meet with a pastor in his church for spiritual counsel. The appointment was made by telephone. Before hanging up, the pastor asked the man to make sure that when he came he brought his checkbook. "I did not know that I had to pay to see you," the man said. "You don't," replied the pastor. "I simply want to see where your priorities lie!" When we consider the biblical pattern, we discover that our giving should be directed to the work of the gospel and the support of our Christian brothers and sisters and the poor as represented in the needs of the widows and orphans.

BLATANT AND SUBTLE FORMS OF STEALING

When we trace stealing to its roots, we discover ugly twins, namely greed and selfishness. One of my colleagues in ministry was a partner with Arthur Andersen before being called to the ministry. When we travel together I often ask him to tell me stories from the old days when he had a "real job"! On one occasion he recounted a partner's meeting which was addressed by the man who followed Arthur Anderson as the head of the organization. By this time Leonard Spacek was elderly and infirm, but his word of warning reverberated around the walls of the boardroom. In stressing the importance of being wise stewards of financial resources, he called his successors to beware of one thing in particular, namely greed. He had seen it kill an organization, and he was not so foolish as to think that the same powerful monster could not swallow his beloved Arthur Andersen. Mercifully he is not alive to discover that at least in some measure his warning had proved prophetic in the financial disaster of the scandal which has led to the collapse of the company. How subtle this can be. The successful business executive who would never think of stealing a dozen golf balls from the pro shop at his country club may still be willing to fudge the figures for the accountants to ensure an inflated stock price which will be to his benefit.

God detests such theft, and the Old Testament prophets declared his anger:

Hear this, you who trample the needy
    and do away with the poor of the land,
    saying,
"When will the New Moon be over
    that we may sell grain,
and the Sabbath be ended
    that we may market wheat?"—
skimping the measure,
    boosting the price
    and cheating with dishonest scales,
buying the poor with silver
    and the needy for a pair of sandals . . .
        —AMOS 8:4–6

God had made provision for the poor in His Law, and for the employer to act in this way was to take what had been entrusted to another by God Himself. They were selling even the sweepings that should have been left for the poor to gather. Employers steal from their workers when they fail to pay them an adequate wage. The businessman steals from his clients when he inflates the value of his goods or services or when he fails to give fair value for the money he's receiving. A biblical business ethic demands that in buying and selling we do not take advantage of one another. This is one way for a Christian to obey the command of Jesus to be salt and light in the middle of a crooked and perverse generation. Instead of scheming deceitfully and offering an inferior product for the price of one that is better, the Christian businessman will tell the truth and trust his heavenly Father with the outcome.

Recent surveys reveal that American workers admit, without shame, that they spend more than 20 percent of their time at work "goofing off." That means that they are only working four days a week. They are being paid for five days, but they are working four. Almost half of those interviewed admitted to chronic malingering and calling in sick even when they were healthy. In each instance they were stealing their employer's time and money.

As employees we are stealing when we use the telephone to waste time or to make disallowed personal calls. We steal when we invent our expense accounts rather than reporting our expenditures accurately. We steal when the office supplies find their way into our children's school bags.

How many of us have books or tapes or compact discs that we have borrowed and never returned? We may have accepted the loan with every intention of returning it. But now so much time has elapsed that we decide to keep the item. In doing so, our borrowing has become theft. When we fail to return property we have borrowed, we steal. One of the marks of the wicked, the psalmist, tells us is that they "borrow and do not repay" (Psalm 37:21).

We steal when we make insurance claims that are fraudulent or exaggerated. Every insurance agent tells us that part of the reason for the high cost of our premiums may be traced to dishonesty on a massive scale.

Failure to put our religion into practice by supporting our needy parents and grandparents is a form of theft, and when we try and justify our negligence we are partners with him who destroys (Proverbs 28:24). There is something particularly distasteful when the theft involves family members, as in the case of Jacob's theft of a blessing which by right belonged to his brother Esau (Genesis 27).

And what about stealing another's reputation by invading their purity or slandering their name? A sixteenth-century preacher faced with a woman who confessed to being a slanderer asked her, "Do you frequently fall into this fault?" "Yes, very often," the woman replied. "Your fault is great but God's mercy is greater," said the preacher. "Go to the nearest market and purchase a freshly killed chicken still covered with its feathers. You will then walk a certain distance, plucking the bird as you go along. When you finish your work return to me here."

The woman did as the preacher instructed and returned, anxious for an explanation. "Ah," said the preacher, "you've been faithful to the first part of my instructions. Now retrace your steps and gather up all the feathers you have scattered." "But I can't" protested the woman. "I cast them carelessly on every side and the wind carried them in every direction. How can I ever recover them?" "And so it is with your words of slander," said the preacher. "Like the feathers, they have been scattered and cannot be recalled. Go and sin no more."

The severe impact of such theft is illustrated in the life of David Livingstone. In the early days when Livingstone was exploring Africa, he left his wife home in Great Britain. He wanted to safeguard her from some of the hardships while he prepared a place for her to join him. Meanwhile, however, back in Britain, people began to talk unkindly, suggesting that there was a problem in the Livingstone's relationship, which there never was. They said so many unkind things that were troubling to Livingstone that he sent for his wife prematurely. She became ill and died. By their slanderous tongues those people stole from David Livingstone. They stole his reputation, they stole his wife, and they stole from his ministry.

In Shakespeare's *Othello*, one of the characters, Iago, declares:

> *Good name in man and woman, dear my lord,*
> *Is the immediate jewel of their souls:*

Who steals my purse steals trash . . .
But he that filches from me my good name
Robs me of that which not enriches him
And makes me poor indeed. (3.3.)

If I were to have tried to pass off that quote as my own, then I would have been guilty of another form of stealing, that is, plagiarism. The Internet has provided a unique opportunity for students to steal and then present as their own the intellectual property of others. In doing so the thief seeks to elevate himself and cares nothing for the good of his neighbor.

In each of these instances the thief fails to acknowledge that in this commandment we are forbidden "to pant after the possessions of others." Calvin aptly summarizes what this commandment forbids:

> *We will duly obey this commandment, then, if, content with our lot, we are zealous to make only honest and lawful gain; if we do not seek to become wealthy through injustice, nor attempt to deprive our neighbor of his goods to increase our own; if we do not strive to heap up riches cruelly wrung from the blood of others; if we do not madly scrape together from everywhere, by fair means or foul, whatever will feed our avarice or satisfy our prodigality.* (Institutes, 409)

But what about the positive side of this commandment? It should be obvious. We must do whatever we can for the good of our neighbor. We must work faithfully to help each person keep what belongs to him or her. Our duty is, as Jesus said, to treat others, as we would like them to treat us. "In everything, do to others what you would have them do to you, for this sums up the Law and the Prophets" (Matthew 7:12). The apostle John informs his readers that one of the identifying marks of genuine Christian experience is love for our brothers. He then points out the incongruity of belief minus behavior. "If anyone has material possessions and sees his brother in need but has no pity on him, how can the love of God be in him?" (1 John 3:17).

Since we are stewards of all that we have, we must employ our possessions to share with those in need. We cannot claim to be adequately obeying this command by fulfilling the negative aspect alone. We are to be those who, in Isaiah's words, are spending ourselves on behalf of the hungry and seeking to satisfy the needs of the oppressed. Evangelical Christianity is at best "patchy" when it comes to taking seriously this injunction. The reason the thief is to start using his hands productively, says Paul, is not in order that he can feel better about himself or herself but in order that he "may have something to share with those in need" (Ephesians 4:28).

Luke 19:1–10 provides us with a wonderful illustration of this in the story of a big change in a little man. Was it curiosity alone that caused Zacchaeus to climb the tree so that he could see who Jesus was? Had the word spread about the change that had taken place in a fellow tax collector named Levi? Is it possible that Zacchaeus' conscience had begun to bother him and he found himself acknowledging that he could not continue to live as a thief? Maybe it was learning about Christ's compassion that drew him to find a vantage point above the crowds.

How different compassion would be to the response of organized religion, which was represented, in the grim, harsh teachers of the Law, who refused to give him the time of day. But Jesus—He comes for the least and the last and the left out. By this time, in Luke's gospel, we have almost come to expect that the eyes of Christ, out of which heaven itself seemed to look upon earth, will fasten, not on the religious leaders or upon those struggling to gain His attention, but instead upon this unlikely recipient of His grace and favor. Jesus is the Good Shepherd who leaves the ninety-nine and searches the hillside for the lost one (Luke 15:3–7). It is not the healthy who need a doctor, but the sick, and Jesus came not to call the righteous but sinners to repentance (Mark 2:17; Luke 19:10). Christ was on His way to Jerusalem to shed His blood for the undeserving. If that were not the case, what hope would there have been for you and me?

Jesus calls Zacchaeus by name and informs him that it is imperative that He stay at his house today. The reason, of course, is given in Luke 19:10: "For the Son of Man came to seek and to save what was lost." And this little man was lost. Wealthy he may be, but certainly not in terms of friends. From the outside, he probably appeared quite secure and self-satisfied. But underneath that superficial level, the reality was known to Zacchaeus and to Jesus. As the murmurs of anger and disappointment run through the crowd, Zacchaeus gladly welcomed Jesus to his home.

We have no record of the private conversation that took place behind closed doors. Luke describes for us the transformation that has taken place in this man's life. The robber has become the giver. The cheat has been changed! Can't you just see this little man wrestling with the wonder of it all? "I went there to that roadside and climbed the tree hoping for a glimpse of this Jesus. Apparently He came to Jericho looking expressly *for me!*" Edersheim writes of this: "In that dim twilight of the new day, and at this new creation, the angels sang and the sons of God shouted together, and all was melody and harmony in his heart."

Zacchaeus knew the Law, and he stood before it guilty. Each of us by nature is in the same predicament. We all stand guilty before the mirror of the Law. Each of us needs to discover what dawned upon this little man in his encounter with Jesus. In this Jesus there was forgiveness, the cleansing of his guilty conscience, a clean page in the journal of his life, a fresh start, a new day. Because Jesus was on His way to Jerusalem to die upon the cross for all the cheating and stealing and dark stuff in our lives that we dare hardly admit to ourselves.

As you picture Zacchaeus standing there making this declaration, don't miss the fact that here in an encounter with God's kindness he was led to repentance. He was saying no to the selfishness that had marked his everyday life. He had grasped that he could not hold on to Jesus as his Savior and continue to hold on to the stealing from which Jesus sets him free. It involved him saying no to his secrecy. This encounter was very personal, but it could not stay private. The word would quickly spread. "Do you know that Zacchaeus was just 'round at my house and he repaid me all the money he had stolen, and with interest!" He had looked into the mirror of the Law and realized that he was a thief and a sinner. Then he had looked into the face of the Lord Jesus Christ and cast himself upon His mercy. Then the same Law which had served to condemn him and which could not serve as a means of getting into God's good books became for him a pathway to freedom. As Motyer puts it, "The law of God is the life-style of the redeemed."[5]

So as we seek to obey this commandment, we must consider what we owe our neighbors and should then pay them what we owe. And in this command, as with the others, we must be reminded, as Calvin said, that this rule was established for our hearts as well as for our hands. In this way we will be prevented from the externalism that marked the Pharisees and will instead rejoice to have this law written in our hearts.

9

THE TRUTH MATTERS

You shall not give false testimony against your neighbor.
—EXODUS 20:16

I have learned my lessons. I hope I never tell any lies again. Sometimes you become a prisoner of your own lie. Ultimately I have no excuses."

With that statement, Jonathan Aitken acknowledged that his fall from grace was now complete. The debt collectors took his watch and cufflinks and his son's personal computer from his house in an effort to recoup his outstanding £3 million in legal costs. One of the brightest stars in Britain's conservative party, who had been tipped as a future Prime Minister, was now a shadow of his former self. His political career was over, his marriage had broken down, his considerable fortune was gone, and he had the unhappy distinction of being only one of three people in the twentieth-century forced to resign from the Privy Council. At the age of fifty-six, a reputation he had built over the years was completely destroyed. Why? Because he did not tell the truth. The judge in sentencing him to serve time in prison, said, "For nearly four years you wove a web of deceit in which you entangled yourself and from which there was no way out unless you were prepared to come clean and tell the truth. Unfortunately you were not."

How did it come about that someone who was born to privilege, who had studied at Eton and then Oxford, and who had enjoyed a distinguished career in journalism and then politics should find himself financially bankrupt and morally disgraced? The BBC's Joshua Rozenberg observed, "What started as a little lie snowballed into a criminal lie."

In September of 1993, Aitken, who was then the defense procurement minister for the British government, spent a weekend at the Ritz Hotel in Paris, courtesy of Said Ayas, a businessman with close connections to the Saudi royal family. Motivated presumably by fear or by pride, or by a combination of the two, Aitken falsely claimed that his wife Lolicia had settled the bill. An initial investigation brought no charges against him, and when Prime Minister John Major appointed Aitken to his cabinet, it appeared that the Ritz affair had blown over.

But the Ritz allegations came back stronger than ever. Aitken then decided to sue his media accusers, and in doing so made the grandiose claim, "If it has fallen to my destiny to start a fight to cut out the cancer of bent and twisted journalism in our country with the simple sword of truth and the trusty shield of British fair play, so be it."

When the case once again reached the High Court, Aitken continued to insist that his wife had paid the bill at the Ritz. When evidence was produced that proved that his wife had been in Switzerland and could not have paid the bill, his case collapsed. The evidence also contradicted a signed statement by Mr. Aitken's daughter, Victoria, then seventeen, which supported her father's version of the events. And so he was finally forced to admit that he had committed perjury by claiming under oath that his wife had paid the Ritz bill. He also pleaded guilty to conspiring to prevent the course of justice by drafting a false witness statement under his daughter's name and then getting her to sign it.

Aitken's road to ruin began somewhere on the inside when he failed to join with Agur in seeking God. "Two things I ask of you, O LORD; do not refuse me before I die: Keep falsehood and lies far from me; give me neither poverty nor riches, but give me only my daily bread. Otherwise, I may have too much and disown you and say, 'Who is the LORD?' Or I may become poor and steal, and so dishonor the name of my God" (Proverbs 30:7–9).

Although that case had a high profile and took place on the other side of the Atlantic, the story is not unusual here in America. The words of the prophet Isaiah seem to describe our society only too well: "Justice is driven back, and righteousness stands at a distance; truth has stumbled in the streets, honesty cannot enter. Truth is nowhere to be found, and whoever shuns evil becomes a prey" (Isaiah 59:14–15).

If the statistics on lying are to be believed, then 91 percent of the American population tells lies regularly. The majority of us find it hard to get through a week without lying. One in five can't make it through a single day. Dishonesty, it would seem, is woven into the very fabric of our culture. Deceit runs through our society like so many dark veins through marble. The corridors of political power are plagued by it. The Academy is rife with plagiarism, and organized religion cannot deny the fact that it has significant internal problems with honesty and integrity.

The issue is pervasive, but instead of tackling it as we would a noxious weed in our garden, we mistakenly tolerate it and in certain cases cultivate it. An article from *Child* magazine, in the 1990s, contrasted the "old view," which taught that all lying was bad, with the "new view" that some lying is considered normal. The proponents of this "new view" tell us that parents should not be unduly alarmed by their children's first few lies but should view them as an important step in the "development of self." In striking contrast, the Bible identifies a lying tongue as evidence of our depravity. "Their throats are open graves; their tongues practice deceit. The poison of vipers is on their lips" (Romans 3:13).

The ninth commandment is a call to truthfulness, a commitment to truth that is more than skin deep. God delights in truth in the inward being. Honesty is first and foremost an affair of the heart. Once again, in this commandment, as in all the others, we come face-to-face with ourselves in the mirror of God's Law. The first deception we need to tackle is *self*-deception. Kidding ourselves that we are fine, ignoring the lies and slanders, the broken promises, and the gossip of which we are guilty. "If we claim to be without sin, we deceive ourselves and the truth is not in us" (1 John 1:8).

At the same time the Law functions not only as a mirror but also as a signpost pointing us to the Lord Jesus. Better still, it acts as pedagogue, taking us by the hand and leading us to the truth that sets us free. When we have discovered that by grace we are already in His good books, the Law defines the pattern of our lives. As Alec Motyer puts it, "In Christ the law becomes a minister of life to those who set their feet in its paths."[1] As we study each of these commandments, it is important that we do not lose sight of what we considered at the outset. "The Christian is both 'not under law' (Rom.6:14, *i.e.* as a way of redemption, cf. Rom.8:1–2; Gal.3:13) and yet 'under law' (1 Cor. 9:20) as a divinely authorized pattern of life."[2] A life that is marked by wisdom, joy, light, spiritual energy, and integrity is what David describes in Psalm 19. The laws of God are not irksome to His children. They are precious and sweet. They warn of danger on either side of the path and there is great reward in keeping them (vv. 7–13).

The Law of the Lord is perfect because God is perfect. He cannot lie. He is the God of truth and is made known to us as the *true God*. This is in contrast to the gods who did not make the heavens and the earth and "who will perish from the earth and from under the heavens" (Jeremiah 10:11). Before issuing the first command, God identifies Himself as "I AM." He is the living God, the eternal King who stands in striking contrast to the worthless idols and images that are a fraud; they have no breath in them. It should then be no surprise that those who by grace have become children of the true God should themselves bear the family likeness and be characterized by truth. The Holy Spirit is the Spirit of truth, and Jesus is the truth, and everyone who is on the side of truth listens to Him (John 18:7).

The apostle John concludes his first letter with a warning to stay away from idols. They represent lies, and the believer lives in the realm of what is true. "We know also that the Son of God has come and has given us understanding, so that we may know him who is true. And we are in him who is true—even in his Son Jesus Christ. He is the true God and eternal life" (1 John 5:20).

Stated most simply, the ninth commandment tells us that we must tell the truth at all times. Derek Prime provides a more comprehensive answer: "The ninth commandment forbids in principle all untruth and falsehood, and in particular perjury, and proclaims the necessity of truthfulness of speech."[3] Calvin provides this summary of the purpose of the command:

Let us not malign anyone with slander or false charges, nor harm his substance by falsehood, in short, injure him by un-bridled evilspeaking and impudence. To this prohibition the command is linked that we should faithfully help everyone as much as we can in affirming the truth, in order to protect the integrity of his name and possessions . . . hence this command-ment is lawfully observed when our tongue, in declaring the truth, serves both the good repute and advantage of our neigh-bors." (Institutes, 411, 412)

Solomon tells us that "the LORD detests lying lips, but he delights in all who are truthful" (Proverbs 12:22). We may tell lies or practice deceit with a wink of the eye, a nod of the head, and even by our silence, but we sin most easily in our words. Indeed, says James, it is religious hypocrisy that allows a man to regard himself as holy while failing to "keep a tight rein on his tongue" (James 1:26). If you encounter an individual who has never ever said anything wrong, you have met someone who may legitimately consider himself perfect (James 3:2).

The tongue is a slab of membrane that encloses a complex array of muscles and nerves. We need it to chew, taste, and swallow. Without a tongue, no ambassador can adequately represent our nation, no attorney can represent truth in the courtroom. Without the tongue, our world would be reduced to unintelligible shrugs and grunts. Unlike a saw that becomes blunt with use, the tongue gets sharper and sharper. A scorpion has all its venom in its tail; human beings have all their venom in their tongue.

James describes the devastating impact of the tongue in terms of fire and poison (James 3:1–12). The tongue is a difficult member of the body to tame. Human restraint is ineffective. It will be brought under control only by divine power, the power that raised Jesus from the dead. In the same way that a small spark may set a forest on fire, our tongues are capable of beginning a blaze that will not easily be controlled: "The tongue also is a fire, a world of evil among the parts of the body. It corrupts the whole person, sets the whole course of his life on fire, and is itself set on fire by hell" (James 3:6).

James tells us that the *source* of the destructive power of the tongue is hell. Perhaps when he wrote these words he had in mind the occasion when Jesus confronted His opponents by telling them that they belonged to their father, the devil, who does not hold "to the truth, for there is no truth in him. When he lies, he speaks his native language, for he is a liar and the father of lies" (John 8:44). When the devil, in the form of a serpent, tackled Eve in the garden, he lied to her: "'You will not surely die,' the serpent said to the woman" (Genesis 3:4). Even when Satan uses the truth, it is in order to manipulate it, to multiply untruths, and create chaos and distortion. Behind every word that is unclean, untrue, angry, spiteful, divisive, and unkind is Satan himself.

The impact of this evil is not localized and contained. It follows a *course*. Like blood poisoning, it courses through the whole body. It is not hard to tell one lie, but it is difficult to tell *only* one. Eventually the liar becomes tangled in the web of deceit he has woven. As we grow older, the incapacities of old age may prevent us from some of the sins of our youth. But one problem area that is not neutralized by the process of time is that of the tongue. If we have failed in our earlier days to cultivate truth in our inward being, we may find that our old age is marked by exaggerations, flattery, and a delicious delight in rumor. We may be amazed at the carefree way in which we may sin in this respect time and again. "Those who do not markedly suffer from this disease are rare indeed. We delight in a certain poisoned sweetness experienced in ferreting out and in disclosing the evils of others" (*Institutes*, 412).

James also points out the *force* with which we are faced. When our children were small we enjoyed visiting Sea World. We sat together amazed at the way in which the trainers were able to make the sea lions dance in time, cause the dolphin to capture the rubber rings, and best and most amazing of all, ride around the arena on the back of Shamu the "killer." The irony is, of course, found in the fact that while man is able to tame these giant creatures of the sea, he cannot bring his tongue under control. Since the tongue has the power of life and death (Proverbs 18:21), we need to exercise extreme caution lest we "yield our tongues to evil-speaking and caustic wit and give our minds without cause to sly suspicion" (*Institutes*, 413).

We dare not treat this matter lightly. The Bible pays particular attention to the sins of the tongue. "Therefore each of you must put off falsehood and speak truthfully to his neighbor, for we are all members of one body" (Ephesians 4:25). Unless we are routinely before the mirror of God's Word in a manner that takes care of what we see, we may begin to tolerate half-truths, flattery, gossip, and caustic, harmful comments and thereby poison the life of our community. One wrong word may spoil a character, smear a reputation, and mar the usefulness of a life. Part of what it means to love our neighbor is that we are absolutely truthful in what we say *to* and *about* them.

TRUTH IN COURT

In the Aitken case the father asked his daughter to say what was untrue in order to safeguard his interests. To take a solemn oath proclaiming that only the truth, the whole truth, and nothing but the truth will be told and then to fail to do so is to be guilty of lying in its most blatant form. When this command was given, many crimes carried the death penalty. This meant that when someone deliberately misrepresented the truth under oath it could result in the execution of the accused. The laws of justice and mercy were very specific and provided the foundation upon which the laws of Great Britain and the United States were built. False reports were forbidden, and no help was to be given to a wicked man by being a malicious witness. Solomon describes the harm that is done by a false witness: "Like a club or a sword or a sharp arrow is the man who gives false testimony against his neighbor" (Proverbs 25:18). This command also forbids the taking of a bribe, as it "blinds those who see and twists the words of the righteous" (Exodus 23:8).

For many of us, our first real insight into the workings of the United States criminal justice system was when we were treated to (or inflicted with) the gavel-to-gavel coverage of the O. J. Simpson trial. Irrespective of our views on the verdict, there will have been few of us who found that it bolstered our confidence in the system. I found myself unsettled, feeling like the psalmist when he declared, "Surely in vain have I kept my heart pure; in vain have I washed my hands in innocence. . . . When I tried to understand all this, it was oppressive to me till I entered the sanctuary of God; then I understood their final destiny" (Psalm 73:13, 16–17). God has promised that the deceitfulness of the false witness will not go unpunished: "A false witness will not go unpunished, and he who pours out lies will perish" (Proverbs 19:9). While in the short run the perjurer may apparently go "scot free," the final accounts have yet to be settled.

"Acquitting the guilty and condemning the innocent—the
LORD detests them both" (Proverbs 17:15).

THE SIN OF SLANDER

If this commandment only addressed the matter of perjury, then most of us would be ready to move on. After all,
we may never have faced the courtroom scene but feel ourselves ready should that day arrive. But this commandment
tackles us in the ebb and flow of life at home, in the community, and at church. It is here that we come face-to-face
with our proneness to engage in false judgments and unfair
criticism, to use flattery, and to join the harmful whisperers'
society that trades in juicy rumors.

Here, I think, is a case in point of what we mentioned in
the prologue about the tendency to set aside the commandments in favor of our own external rules and regulations. A
church may be more rigid on its man-made by-laws, which
address the issues of playing cards, cigars, movies, and
ladies' makeup, than it is on God's Law, which in this case
forbids the toleration of gossip and slander. The spirit of the
Pharisee that hides behind the smoke screen of comparative
obedience ("I thank you that I am not like all other men,"
Luke 18:11) is not unknown in evangelical circles. We must
be on our guard lest we fall into the trap of prohibiting what
God allows or allowing what God prohibits. The ninth commandment leaves us in no doubt that God prohibits falsehood of any kind, and so when we find it lurking in the
corridors of our minds we must ask it to leave immediately.

Peter urged his readers to "love one another deeply from
the heart" (1 Peter.1:22). He longed for them to grow up in
their salvation as God's Word nourished them. In that context he gave them this charge: "Therefore, rid yourselves of

196

all malice and all deceit, hypocrisy, envy, and slander of every kind" (1Peter 2:1). He might equally well have said: "Keep the ninth commandment!"

It is a good discipline to test our speech by asking of what we are about to say, especially when it concerns another person. Is it *kind?* Is it *true?* Is it *necessary?* Slander usually fails in all three counts but sometimes only on two. Just because a thing is true does not mean that we have the right to report it. When we engage in slander, we defame others and seek to exalt ourselves. Those who indulge in the habit of running down their neighbors by making false statements or by enjoying lies and false reports are guilty of slander. Stirred by hatred or jealousy, the slanderer gathers little groups in the corner of the room. There, often under the pharisaical disguise of "a matter for prayer," he passes on confidential tidbits of information that are calculated to destroy the reputation of those who are not there to defend themselves. It is incongruous for a believer to go about spreading slander, for lies and deceit are Satan's domain. It is dangerous to injure people with our tongues, for we will be judged for all our careless words.

GOSSIP

"A perverse man stirs up dissension, and a gossip separates close friends" (Proverbs 16:28). Sadly, most of us know this to be true from personal experience. We have lost respect for a friend when someone, who probably should have remained silent, reported to us what this friend had said about us in our absence. Pascal wrote, "I lay it as a fact that if all men knew what others say of them, there would not be four friends in the world." Solomon identifies the peculiar enticement to engage in gossip. "The words of a gossip are like choice morsels; they go down to a man's inmost parts" (Proverbs 18:8). The magazine racks in the grocery store are bulging with stories that are full of such "choice morsels" tempting us to bite. In the hallways of our churches we may hear the sound bites that are the stuff of gossip.

"I heard that he was living with his girlfriend."

"Apparently he owes a lot and refuses to pay."

"Somebody said that she's his third wife."

We must learn to break the gossip chain. "He who covers over an offense promotes love, but whoever repeats the matter separates close friends" (Proverbs 17:9). "It would be difficult to estimate how many friendships are broken, how many reputations ruined, and the peace of how many homes destroyed through careless gossip often indulged in for the lack of something better to do," Randolf Tasker rightly observed. When we find ourselves on the receiving end of gossip, we can build a firewall by asking the person whether we can quote him, or by stating that we have no interest in participating in untruthful talk. We do well to observe the wisdom contained in this rhyme by William Norris:

If your lips would keep from slips,

Five things observe with care:

To whom you speak; of whom you speak;

And how, and when, and where.

RUMOR

Rumor is a close cousin of gossip. In *King Henry IV,* Shakespeare observes:

Rumor is a pipe
Blown by surmises, jealousies, conjectures,
And of so easy and so plain a stop
That the blunt monster with uncounted heads,
The still-discordant wavering multitude,
Can play upon it.

Like the woman we met in chapter 8, we cannot recover the "feathers" of rumor and gossip once they have been spread. The winds of slander take the rumor far beyond our reach to stop it. Chuck Swindoll pictures rumor as "a monstrous giant, capable of prying open more caskets, exposing more closet skeletons and stirring up more choking scandalous dust than any other tool on earth."[4]

FLATTERY AND EXAGGERATION

If gossip is saying something behind a person's back that we would never say to his face, then flattery is saying to a person's face what we would never say behind his back. In other words, it is insincere and false speaking which is harmful to our neighbor. Proverbs says that the flatterer spreads a net for the feet of his unsuspecting victims. Flattery is like perfume. Sniff it, maybe, but whatever you do, don't swallow it! We dare not regard this as rather harmless. God does not. Psalm 12 tells us that the Lord will cut off all flattering lips! When we cultivate this kind of talk, it soon becomes apparent that we are superficial and that our words carry little weight. Our conversation should be full of grace and seasoned with salt (Colossians 4:6). It was a mark of the preaching of Paul and his colleagues that they never used flattery.

When we exaggerate, we distort the truth. Sometimes

we exaggerate in order to curry favor with a person. We are tempted to tell our supervisor that his talk to the staff was "the best we have ever heard." If in our heart of hearts we really thought that it was marginal, then we are lying and the form in which we serve up our deceit is exaggerated talk. We may also exaggerate in order to impress. When we are asked how our game of golf turned out, we say, "I never missed a fairway all day." It would be more truthful to say, "On five out of eighteen holes I was in the fairway." When someone exaggerates on our behalf and we fail to correct them because the false impression they've created feeds our ego, we are guilty of falsehood.

We will be saved from much of this by a commitment to let our yes mean yes and our no mean no. If we are careless with the facts in assuring a client of a delivery date for a product or in describing the benefit of a product, we will all too quickly slip into a pattern where our vagueness becomes a form or deceit. Parents need to be especially careful of this with their children. We must train our children to be careful with the facts. If a thing happened in the street and when they relate it they say it happened in the backyard, we should not let it pass. It is important to correct them, for there is no telling where deviation from the truth will end. The maxim mentioned in an earlier chapter applies here too.

Sow a thought—reap an action.

Sow an action—reap a habit.

Sow a habit—reap a character.

Sow a character—reap a destiny.

What prompts us to lie in these various ways?

We have already traced the origin to the wickedness of our hearts (Luke 6:44–45), but what are the secondary causes? We tell lies about our achievements because we are jealous of another's success and want to appear at least equal to them, if not better than them. We tell lies because we are angry and want to harm our opponents. We tell lies to cover up our mistakes and misdeeds. We tell lies because we are trying to impress someone and the facts alone are not enough, so we embellish them. We may tell lies out of a desire for revenge. In summary, there are essentially two things that underlie our breaking of the ninth commandment—pride and fear. The answer to both is in the cross.

When I survey the wondrous cross,

On which the Prince of glory died,

My richest gain I count but loss

and pour contempt on all my pride.

What have I to dread, what have I to fear,

Leaning on the everlasting arms?

The wonder of the gospel is this—that all of our lies and deception have been laid on Him who perfectly obeyed the truth. When He died upon the cross, we were the beneficiaries of His obedience. As Skip Ryan puts it, "All the merit of Christ, who perfectly kept the law, perfectly obeyed the truth, is given to you. You give Him all the filthy rags of your lies. He who never lied hung on the cross as a liar. When God looks at you and me, He sees the perfect righteousness of Christ's truth-keeping."[5] It is this liberating and

201

energizing truth that establishes our identity and enables us to "faithfully help everyone as much as we can in affirming the truth, in order to protect the integrity of his name and possessions" (*Institutes*, 411).

We began this book by noting Nelson's call to the members of the English fleet to do their duty. We said that it was akin to the call of Christ to His followers. It is important that we remind ourselves continually that we do not *keep ourselves* in God's good books by our *duty*.

> *Since God has secured his love for me completely through my union with Jesus, my own attitude should change about my performance of the duties God requires. I should recognize that doing my duty cannot secure any more of the love that he offers, since that love and the means of securing it are complete in Christ's work. This awareness takes the energy-sapping, heart-mutilating striving for God's affection from my life. The paths of obedience lead me to where I understand that love more fully, but they provide no more of God's love. If my striving were what made God love me more, then when the Holy Spirit eventually showed me that my best works are filthy rags, I would be forced for ever to doubt that I had much of God's love. As a result, I would always question his care. Yea, because of my union with Christ, I need never doubt that I am fully loved, even as the husks of my sin cling to me.*[6]

POSTSCRIPT

"'I tell you the truth, it is hard for a rich man to enter the kingdom of heaven. Again I tell you, it is easier for a camel to go through the eye of a needle than for a rich man to enter the kingdom of God.' When the disciples heard this, they were greatly astonished and asked, 'Who then can be saved?' Jesus looked at them and said, 'With man this is impossible, but with God all things are possible'" (Matthew 19:23–26).

Jonathan Aitken's perjury trial opened this chapter. We close it with the wonderful news that he is now a Christian. My wife and I were introduced to him at a function in Washington, D.C. His testimony of God's grace in his life is humble and radiant. Among other projects, he is currently writing the authorized biography of Chuck Colson!

10

THE OTHER MAN'S GRASS

You shall not covet your neighbor's house. You shall not covet your neighbor's wife, or his manservant or maidservant, his ox or donkey, or anything that belongs to your neighbor.

—EXODUS 20:17

*M*agnetic Resonance Imaging is a medical diagnostic technique that creates images of the body using the principles of nuclear magnetic resonance. A versatile, powerful, and sensitive tool, an MRI can generate thin-section images of any part of the body—including the heart, arteries, and veins—from any angle and direction, without surgical invasion and in a relatively short period of time. It can also creates "maps" of biochemical compounds within any cross section of the human body. These maps give basic biomedical and anatomical information that provides new knowledge and may allow early diagnosis of disease.[1]

I wonder if Hebrews had been written today whether the writer might not have used this imagery instead of a double-edged sword in referring to the penetrating power of the Word of God. In the same way that an MRI is able to reveal what is not immediately obvious from the outside, so too the Word of God penetrates deeply and reveals our true condition. "Nothing in all creation is hidden from God's sight. Everything is uncovered and laid bare before the eyes of him to whom we must give account" (Hebrews 4:13). We have grown accustomed to think of the Bible as a mirror which shows us what we are like. The tenth commandment is a forcible reminder that even our thoughts and desires do not escape God's attention.

"The tenth commandment is perhaps the most revealing and devastating of all the commandments, for it deals explicitly with the inward nature of the law. Covetousness is an attitude of the inward nature which may or may not express itself in an outward acquisitive act."[2] Coveting is distinct from the other nine commandments. Each of them involves observable behavior, but a covetous heart may not be immediately obvious to others because it is *totally* inward. Although this is the final commandment, it is basic to the others. It leaves us in no doubt that, like covetousness, the various sins forbidden in the previous commands originate in the heart (Mark 7:21–23). "The heart is deceitful above all things and beyond cure. Who can understand it?" (Jeremiah 17:9). The psalmist recognizes that he needs to be forgiven and cleansed from hidden or secret faults (Psalm 19:12).

We may manage to convince ourselves that we are innocent of stealing, murder, and adultery, but when we come to this command, we find, as Calvin says, that it "provides God with a sharper lancet for not only sounding the bottom of our heart, but all our thoughts and imaginations. Everything within us becomes exposed and brought to consciousness."[3] This was the experience of the apostle Paul that he describes in Romans 7. Although he was particularly careful in keeping the Law, it was the inwardness of the tenth commandment that brought him to his knees. Later, when he wrote to the Colossians, he pointed out that covetousness is a form of idolatry because it puts the object of desire in the place of God (Colossians 3:5).

According to the *Oxford English Dictionary*, covetousness is the inordinate and culpable desire of possessing that which belongs to another or to which one has no right. In other words, it refers to illegitimate desire. Every desire that rises in our hearts is not to be equated with coveting. For instance, when a man desires a wife he desires a good thing, and if he finds her, he receives favor from the Lord (Proverbs 18:22). The desire of parents for children is a desire to receive gifts from the Lord (Psalm 127:4). The desire to exercise spiritual leadership in the church is a God-given desire (1 Timothy 3:1). There are many such things that may be the object of legitimate desire. However, in the instances just mentioned, it is possible that they could become the occasion of coveting. When, for example, our desire for children is driven by jealousy or becomes the occasion of idolatry because we love the thought of children more than we trust God to do what He deems best. Lawful desire can very quickly become coveting when we desire the wrong things, such as our neighbor's wife, or when our desires spring from the wrong motives, for example, to simply get rich.

The Westminster Shorter Catechism summarizes the instruction of the tenth commandment in this way: "The tenth commandment requireth full contentment with our own condition, with a right and charitable frame of spirit toward our neighbor, and all that is his. . . . [and] forbiddeth all discontentment with our own estate, envying or grieving at the good of our neighbor, and all inordinate notions and affections to anything that is his." As we have walked along this "pathway to freedom," we have been left in no doubt about the direct applicability of each of the commandments to our lives. But nowhere perhaps is this more obvious than here where we find ourselves faced with the questions of genuine satisfaction and true contentment. Whatever else may be said about our culture, we could never claim that one of its hallmarks is contentment.

Some years ago I was playing golf with three men, all of them new acquaintances to me. Each of the men was a stockbroker, responsible for significant portfolios. In the course of our conversation that day, I was bold enough to inquire, "How many of your clients would you say are contented?" My question was met by silence. Finally one of them said, "I cannot think of a single client who is contented." They all agreed. This is hardly surprising. Covetousness is not considered a sin in our culture. In my files I have an advertisement that appeared in the *Wall Street Journal* in October 1983. It was a full-page ad headed, "DEMORALIZE THY NEIGHBOR." This ad for Aston Martin automobiles played masterfully on the envious, greedy instincts in each of us. The copy read:

> *It's one thing to trundle by in a Bentley, Jaguar, or Mercedes. Everyone in your neighborhood has one of those. It's quite another thing to come in for a landing in your Lagonda. Get an Aston Martin and demoralize your neighbor.*

Our society thrives on materialism, cashing in on the sin of covetousness. Its modus operandi is to create within our hearts a longing for things we do not have. Not only a longing, but also an attitude of need and entitlement. We need it. We deserve it. Especially if someone else has it.

A few years ago a colleague and I were returning from a missionary conference in France. We had an overnight in

London, and in the evening we walked through the fashion-
able shopping district. In a shop window on New Bond
Street there was a minimal display of clothing which was set
in the context of "The Ten Commandments of Rossini," an
Italian fashion designer. They read as follows:

POWER
EGO
MONEY
PERFECTION
STYLE
TASTE
SOPHISTICATION
SERVICE
LUXURY
COMFORT

Covetousness, of course, is not a new phenomenon. In
the Old Testament we read of a man called Achan who left his
mark in history on account of his covetousness. The Lord had
given strict instructions to the people concerning the devoted
things. These articles of silver and gold and bronze and iron
were sacred to the Lord and were to be put in His treasury.
But Achan stole some items and buried them in the ground
inside his tent. When his sin was exposed he confessed,
"When I saw in the plunder a beautiful robe from Babylonia,
two hundred shekels of silver and a wedge of gold weighing
fifty shekels, I coveted them and took them" (Joshua 7:21). If
he had been contented with what he had, then he could have
admired those things without stealing. The process is clear.
What he *saw* prompted the *desire of his heart* and he *wanted*
these things so much that *stealing* followed. Internally, where

no one else could see, he must have hatched and nurtured a greedy, discontented spirit. He is not alone.

Gehazi was the servant of Elisha the man of God, and he was greedy. This became obvious to more than himself on the day that Naaman was healed of his leprosy. This commander of the army of the king of Aram was so grateful to Elisha that he urged the man of God to accept a gift. Elisha said an emphatic, "No, thank you." He could not accept the offer without compromising the integrity of what had taken place. Gehazi, on the other hand, had no such scruples. He felt that his master had let Naaman off too easy. And so he determined, "I will run after him and get something from him" (2 Kings 5:20).

Once again, the pattern is clear. In his thought-life, known only to God and himself, the destructive process begins. By his own evil desire, he is dragged away and enticed. Instead of focusing on the wonderful change that Naaman discovered, Gehazi's mind was riveted to the chance that Elisha had (from his perspective) squandered. Read the story for yourself, and in it you will find a classic example of what James describes: "Then, after desire has conceived, it gives birth to sin; and sin, when it is full-grown, gives birth to death" (James 1:15). The story is as up-to-date as the breaking news on the Internet.

Greed is no respecter of persons. Some have suggested that it has reached epidemic proportions among the baby boomers, who had in the sixties rejected the materialism of their parents but by the nineties had sold out. This is borne out in this tongue-in-cheek quote from Joe Queenan: "Baby Boomers honestly believe that self-indulgence is okay if it is herbal, organic and all-natural, and that greed is acceptable if it includes a cognate self-actualizing component. In fact, greed is only okay if it is naked and predatory. Camouflaged greed can only lead to bad things like moderate Republicanism."[4]

The "Gehazi syndrome," covetousness, is a silent killer. It blinds the individual to everything he has. Covetousness sees only what he does not have. Take two youngsters who are best friends throughout their school years. They spend overnights at each other's homes. They do their homework together. They graduate from high school and go on to college where both do well. But after college one of them orbits into financial success while the other progresses on a slower track. Envy rears its ugly head, and before you know it, the one with the covetous heart can't stand the success of the other. Instead of loving his neighbor as himself and thereby wanting the best for him, the friend opens the door to malice and resentment, and a friendship is destroyed.

Consider how many families are, on account of covetousness, set at odds with each other at the reading of their father's will. As someone has said, "When there is an inheritance, 99 percent of the people become wolves." When greed grips a man's mind, he is always asking of a situation, "What's best for me?" When selfishness becomes an ingrained pattern of thinking and living, we should not be surprised when old age merely serves to exacerbate the problem.

> It is commonly said that covetousness is one of the reigning sins
> of old age. How strange that it should be so! Especially consid-
> ering what they have seen, and known, and it may be, felt of
> the emptiness and uncertainty of riches. They have witnessed
> how often they make themselves wings. What! And not yet
> convinced! What! Almost at the end of thy journey, and yet
> loading thyself with thick clay! Think of the time of day. It is al-
> most night; even sunset. And art thou mindful of the grave?
> The body is bending downwards, let the heart be upwards.[5]

Although the language is somewhat archaic, the message is clear. When we factor death and eternity into the equation, we begin to see just how foolish it is to fall in love with the world and the things of the world (1 John 2:16). In Luke's gospel we have the record of a dispute between two brothers. For some reason one had all the inheritance and didn't want to give it up. The brother who didn't have any wanted his fair share. Jesus responded to their request for arbitration by issuing a warning and telling a story. "Watch out! Be on your guard against all kinds of greed; a man's life does not consist in the abundance of his possessions" (Luke 12:15).

Both brothers were greedy. One wanted to keep all he had and the other wanted to get all he could. Jesus may well have had in mind the tenth commandment when he warned them that they must be on guard against *all kinds* of greed. A covetous heart may focus on our neighbor's wife, home, employees, and possessions.

It is vital that we learn to ward off the encroachments of a greedy, envious heart. In this we will be helped by recognizing that a man's real life in no way depends upon the number of his possessions. This challenges the prevailing mood of so much of our society. Power and influence, prestige and recognition are more tightly tied to possessions than we are prepared to admit. The problem with the farmer in the story told by Jesus was not that he was successful, nor that he was dishonest, for there is no indication of that. His problem lay in the fact that he was banking in the wrong place. Barclay summarizes his predicament in two phrases. He never saw beyond himself and he never saw beyond this world. He failed to see the emptiness and ultimate futility of such an earth-bound perspective.

Whoever loves money never has money enough;
> whoever loves wealth is never satisfied with his income.
> This too is meaningless.
As goods increase,
> so do those who consume them.
And what benefit are they to the owner
> except to feast his eyes on them?

The sleep of a laborer is sweet,
> whether he eats little or much,
but the abundance of a rich man
> permits him no sleep.
>   —ECCLESIASTES 5:10–12

He will not have any more life when he has much, or any less life when he has little. But covetousness blinds a man to the fact that life is much more important than food and the body more important than clothes.

In my conversation with the stockbrokers at the golf club, I quoted Paul's words to Timothy, "Godliness with contentment is great gain." They had never heard that and wanted to know what it meant and how it worked. And so I tried my best to answer. I told them that the word for contentment which Paul used (*autarkeia*) was a favorite of the stoic philosophers. They thought of contentment in terms of self-sufficiency, but when Paul used the word, he was referring to a contentment that was founded in the provision of our heavenly Father, who knows our needs and in turn supplies what's best for us. The hymn writer puts it succinctly:

Day by day, and with each passing moment,

Strength I find to meet my trials here;

Trusting in my Father's wise bestowment,

I've no cause for worry or for fear.

"Our contentment needs to be not in what we expect others to give, or what we may strive after, but in what God unfailingly provides for us by one means or another."[6] Paul addressed the issue in light of the two fixed points in between which life is lived, our birth and our death.

ARRIVAL

We brought absolutely nothing with us when we entered this world. This is an undeniable fact. I have been present in the delivery room for three births and have listened to the details of countless others, and in no instance did the babies arrive clutching little packages! Job summarized it: "Naked I came from my mother's womb" (Job 1:21). We made a possessionless entry!

DEPARTURE

"And naked I will depart" (Job 1:21). There are no pockets in a shroud. But of course we have dressed death up, and partly in an attempt to deny its grim reality and dreadful finality we plan to be sent off in our Sunday best. So there are a few pockets after all. Once again, the baby boomers have excelled in finding ways to hide from the reality of it all. For us it is a flight of fancy with only two pieces of hand luggage allowed!

Funerals are no longer somber rituals where we pay our respects to the dead. They are cabaret. They are parties, funfests, or what used to be known as happenings. *They entail light shows, productions numbers, props. They include professionally printed programs complete with sound and lighting credits. They involve the screening of buoyant farewell films comprising inept footage of birthday parties and college graduations that was never supposed to be shown in a solemn ceremony. It is no secret that baby boomers have a hard time dealing with death.[7]*

Our lives are lived between these two fixed points. If we are to say no to covetousness, we must learn to say yes to contentment. This involves learning to be content with what we have (Hebrews 13:5). Much of our discontentment may be traced to expectations that are essentially selfish and more often than not completely unrealistic. Paul sets the expectations at a most basic level when he tells Timothy that as far as physical things are concerned, it is sufficient for us to keep our bodies fed and clothed.

A covetous heart never has enough and consequently lives with discontent. On one occasion Rockefeller, the founder of the Standard Oil Company of Ohio and a very wealthy man, was asked by a reporter, "How much money does it take to be happy?" He replied, "Just a little bit more."

Jerome K. Jerome addressed this issue in his book *Three Men in a Boat,* first published in 1889 and still in print. As the three men prepare for their boat trip, it quickly becomes apparent that the upper reaches of the river Thames would not allow for the navigation of a boat large enough to carry all the "stuff" they regarded as indispensable for their journey. Having torn up their first list, they are struck by the wisdom of George when he suggests that they are going about things the wrong way,

"We must not think of the things we could do with, but only of the things we can't do without." The writer observes that this wisdom applies not only to their voyage but also with reference to our trip up the river of life. "How many people, on that voyage, load up the boat until it is in danger of swamping with a load of foolish things which they think essential to the pleasure and comfort of the trip, but which are really only useless lumber."[8]

Paul is not issuing a call to poverty, nor even to a level of simplicity which when exceeded equals sin. He has particular warnings for "the haves" (1 Timothy 6:17), but it is clear that whatever exceeds the basics of food and clothing may be gratefully received and enjoyed. Luxuries (everything beyond food, clothes, and shelter) must never be regarded as necessities. "Better the little that the righteous have than the wealth of many wicked" (Psalm 37:16). Contentedness is not found in piling up added securities besides the daily necessities of food and clothing.

In Shakespeare's *Henry VI, Part 2,* two gamekeepers meet the king in a country place. Failing to recognize, him they ask:

> *"But if thou be a king, where is thy crown?"*
> *"My crown is in my heart, not on my head.*
> *Not deck'd with diamonds and Indian stones*
> *Nor to be seen; my crown is call'd content.*
> *A crown it is that seldom kings enjoy."*

If we are honest, contentment is a crown seldom enjoyed, not just by kings but also by the members of the rank and file. It is a significant moment when the searchlight of God's Word penetrates the selfish preoccupations to which each of us is so prone and allows us to see matters from an eternal perspective. When this happens, the response will not be the same in every case. In each case it will almost inevitably involve the rearrangement of our priorities. In 1998 I received a letter which I have kept on file. It contained a very generous gift to the ministry of Parkside Church, but that was not the reason for keeping it. I kept it as an illustration of how the entrance of God's Word shines light on our priorities.

> *I have been saving for many years to buy a Harley-Davidson*
> *motorcycle. Several weeks ago, however, listening to the sermon*
> *I realized that I should use my financial blessings for God's work*
> *rather than buying a bike in the spring. It dawned on me*
> *through your messages that I would rather be known as a strong*
> *Christian than a businessman who owns a motorcycle, and that*
> *I need to strengthen the former before pursuing the latter.*

I quote this not to make motorcycle owners uncomfortable, but to once again face up to the challenge of this man's example. There are peculiar dangers that accompany a yearning for material riches. We expose ourselves to all sorts of silly and wicked desires that are quite capable of utterly ruining and destroying our souls. The desire for wealth is founded in the illusion that it brings "security." Ironically, it breeds anxiety. The stock market slide is haunting for each one who has tied contentment to more than food and clothes and shelter. When the Beatles began their journey, which proved for a time to be a magical mystery tour, they were unashamed in singing about the fact that *money* was what they wanted. They were not too far down the long and winding road when they realized that money can't buy love, nor can it buy health or lengthen life or evade death.

Money can buy:
Medicine but not health
A house but not a home
Companionship but not friends
Entertainment but not happiness
Food but not an appetite
A bed but not sleep
A good life but not eternal life.

The heart that covets riches will also often crave popularity, power, leisure, and satisfaction. A discontented spirit is vulnerable to temptation. The neighbor's wife will have special appeal for the man who is not delighting himself in the wife of his youth and finding satisfaction in her embrace. Covetousness may prove to be the station from which we catch the train to adultery. We should be in no doubt that although the lure may be freedom, it will prove to be an illusion. Solomon warns against being captivated by an adulteress. "The evil deeds of a wicked man ensnare him; the cords of sin hold him fast" (Proverbs 5:22).

It is not money but the *love of money* that Paul tells us proves to be the root of all kinds of evil (1 Timothy 6:10). How can we tell if our lives are marked by an inordinate desire for riches? Some years ago a friend who is highly successful in his job in the financial markets helped me to answer that question by giving me these points which he had written on the flyleaf of his Bible.

Some telltale signs in the life that is eager for money
Thoughts of money consume my day.
The financial success of others makes me jealous.
I define success in terms of what I *have* rather than what
    I *am* in Christ.

My family is neglected in my pursuit of money.
I close my eyes to the genuine needs of others.
I am prepared to borrow myself into bondage.
I live in the paralyzing fear of losing my money.
I hoard it rather than share it.
God receives my leftovers rather than my first fruits.

"Some people, eager for money, have wandered from the faith and pierced themselves with many griefs" (1 Timothy 6:10). We have already considered Gehazi's tragic end. The list of those who joined him is not short. It includes Ananias and Sapphira, Demas, and one of Jesus' own disciples, Judas Iscariot. One of the great sadnesses in the Christian journey is to see those who "as they go on their way they are choked by life's worries, riches and pleasures, and they do not mature" (Luke 8:14). Let us shudder at the thought of joining their ranks. We must learn to look away to Christ as the only source of true contentment, which is the antidote to covetousness.

There is good reason why the Puritan Jeremiah Burrows titled his book on the mystery of Christian contentment *The Rare Jewel of Christian Contentment*. The very title suggests what we must sadly admit, namely, that contentment is not just unknown by the stockbroker's clients but it is also absent in the lives of too many Christians of lesser wealth. Like the children of Israel, we are all too quickly discontented with God's provision and yearn for the world and its desires (Exodus 16:3; 1 John 2:15–17).

Contentment does not come easily. It is an undervalued virtue, and along with Paul we must *learn* the secret of being content in any and every situation. When the apostle tells us that he can do everything through Christ who gives him strength, he is referring to the fact that *in Christ* he has learned to cope whether he is warm and fed or cold and naked. His contentment is not determined by his circumstances, nor is it discovered in a spirit of detachment; rather, it is learned on the path of duty in his growing relationship with Jesus (Philippians 3:10).

Many of us are tempted to find the key in *doing*, but the answer is actually found in *being*. It is vital that we are routinely humbled by the reminder that the Christian life is grounded, not in what we can *do*, but in what has been *done* for us and what we need done to us. No one has been more help to me in thinking this through than Dr. Sinclair Ferguson. He writes:

> *If* contentment *could be produced by programmed means ("Five steps to contentment in a month") it would be commonplace. Instead, Christians must discover contentment the old-fashioned way: We must* learn *it. Thus we cannot "do" contentment. It is taught by God; we are schooled in it. It is part of the process of being transformed through the renewing of our minds (Romans 12:1–2). It is commanded of us, but paradoxically, it is done to us, not by us. It is not the product of a series of actions but of a renewed and transformed character. Only good trees produce good fruit—and here is the crux of the matter: How do we learn to be content? We must enroll in the divine school in which we are instructed by biblical teaching and providential experience.[9]*

Instead of coveting what God has given to someone else, we must learn to be contented in what our gracious heavenly Father has provided for us. This will not happen in a moment in time. It will take all of our Christian life to learn this lesson. Instead of looking to others to meet our needs, our contentment is to be discovered in learning to live at God's disposal in an ever-deepening relationship with Jesus. Learning to declare from our hearts,

Thou, O Christ, art all I want;

More than all in thee I find.

Or, in more contemporary language:

All that I need is you, Jesus, all that I need is you.

From early in the morning 'til late at night

(and all through the night)

All that I need is you.

The godly Robert Murray McCheyne, who died at the age of twenty-nine while minister of St. Peter's Church in Dundee, Scotland, wrote: "It has always been my ambition to have no plans as regards myself." In keeping with that unusual ambition, one woman wrote: "Years ago I stopped looking to anyone but God to satisfy me. There is no man that can love me enough, no child that can need me enough, no job that can pay me enough, and no experience that can satisfy me enough! Only Jesus."

GOOD NEWS FOR LAWBREAKERS

*Now we know that whatever the law says, it
says to those who are under the law, so that
every mouth may be silenced and the whole
world held accountable to God. Therefore no
one will be declared righteous in his sight by
observing the law; rather, through the law we
become conscious of sin.*

—ROMANS 3:19–20

There is just no way to wriggle out of it. The facts stare
us in the face. None of us can look into the mirror of God's
law and feel good about ourselves. Not if we're honest.
Along with everyone else, we are accountable to God. His
holy standard makes us painfully aware of the fact that we
are lawbreakers.

FACING OUR CONDITION

The Law of God was not given to save us. The Ten Commandments do not serve as a stepladder up which we climb
to heaven. Rather, as we have discovered, God's Law was
given to pinpoint sin, to define it, to bring it out of its hiding place. We are confronted by the seriousness of sin. It is
an offense against God. His Law is broken by our disobedience. By our rebellion we despise His authority. As a result,

we find ourselves alienated and condemned. The wrath of God is "revealed from heaven against all the godlessness and wickedness of men who suppress the truth by their wickedness" (Romans 1:18).

We should not think of God's wrath in terms of the volatile arbitrary outbursts of human emotion. In *The Gospel for Real Life*, Jerry Bridges writes of God's wrath: "This is not the mere petulance of an offended deity because his commands are not obeyed. It is rather the necessary response of God to uphold His moral authority in the universe."[1] This explains statements like these in the Psalms: "The arrogant cannot stand in your presence; you hate all who do wrong" (Psalm 5:5). "God is a righteous judge, a God who expresses his wrath every day" (Psalm 7:11).

The gravity of our condition is brought home to us not simply by realizing the extent of our predicament but by pondering the length to which God went in order to rescue us. Only in the death of the Lord Jesus on behalf of sinners could God's justice be served and God's love conveyed.

GOD'S PROVISION

How deep the Father's love for us

How vast beyond all measure

That He should give His only Son

To make a wretch His treasure.

How deep the pain of searing loss

The Father turns His face away

And wounds that mar the chosen one

Bring many sons to glory.[2]

In this wonderful hymn Stuart Townend captures the essence of God's intervention on behalf of sinners. We stand condemned before the Law, rebels running from a Holy God. What are we to do? What can we do? The apostle Paul answers these questions. Having described the bad news of our condition, he goes on to declare the good news of God's provision.

"*But now* a righteousness from God apart from law has been made known" (Romans 3:21). Here is good news indeed! What we are not able to accomplish, God has accomplished for us. This refers to the perfect righteousness of the Lord Jesus. In His life Jesus obeyed perfectly all the precepts of the Law, and in His death He bore fully all the punishment our sins deserve. In the Cross, sin has been fully dealt with and God has been fully satisfied.

Does this mean that because Jesus died upon the cross men and women are automatically forgiven? The apostle answers that crucial question in the next verse. "This righteousness from God comes through faith in Jesus Christ to *all who believe*" (Romans 3:22). It is by trusting in Him as our Savior that we become the beneficiaries of all that He has accomplished. The essence of this divine transaction is this: "God made Him who had no sin to be sin for us, so that in Him we might become the righteousness of God" (2 Corinthians 5:21). In this great exchange God took our sin and charged it to Christ and took all of His righteousness and credited it to us. "To put it in a very contemporary form, God treated Christ as we deserved to be treated, so that He might treat us as Christ deserved to be treated."[3]

A Personal Response

When we moved to the United States twenty years ago we did something that we had never done in the previous eight years of marriage—we bought a house. It was a new, frightening, wonderful experience involving terminology with which I was to that point unfamiliar. I remember that all of the discussions and inspections led to what is referred to as THE CLOSING. On a particular day the papers were signed and the transaction completed. Becoming a Christian is not dissimilar. In fact the Puritans spoke in terms of "closing" with Christ.

The answer to our condition as lawbreakers is Jesus Christ Himself. It is to come to Him and accept the currency of blood He has offered to purchase our freedom. It means recognizing the futility of attempting to please God by our own good deeds. It involves coming to Him, saying:

Just as I am, without one plea,

But that Thy blood was shed for me,

And that Thou bidd'st me come to Thee,

O Lamb of God, I come! I come!

—Charlotte Elliott (1789–1871)

It remains for me to ask: Do you have a relationship with God through faith in the Lord Jesus Christ? Do you believe in Him? Have you entrusted your life to Him? Are you trusting in Him alone to save you? Have you "closed" with Christ? If so, you will have come to the point of praying:

Lord Jesus Christ, I stand exposed as a lawbreaker. I cannot hide from You; help me to hide in You. All of my efforts to better myself and fulfill the law have proved futile, only You can save me. You have died to bring forgiveness. Forgive me and cleanse me from the guilt and power of sin.

Have you ever prayed like that?

SOME THINGS NEVER CHANGE

God accepts us for Christ's sake and *now* we stand in grace (Romans 5:2). This will always be the case. We do not make ourselves more acceptable to God by avoiding certain sins or performing Christian duties. Every day we are dependent on the perfect righteousness of Christ. As B. B. Warfield wrote:

There is nothing in us or done by us, at any stage of our earthly development, because of which we are acceptable to God. We must always be accepted for Christ's sake, or we cannot be accepted at all. This is not true of us only when we believe. It is just as true after we have believed. It will continue to be true as long as we live. Our need of Christ does not cease with our believing; nor does the nature of our relation to Him or to God through Him ever alter, no matter what our attainments in Christian graces or our achievements in behavior may be. It is always on His "blood and righteousness" alone that we can rest.[4]

So when the devil tempts us to despair by reminding us of the evil in our hearts, we do not respond by listing our achievements but by looking away to Christ and wrapping around ourselves the undeserved robe of righteousness which is ours in Him.

In Christ alone my hope is found

He is my light, my strength, my song.

This cornerstone, this solid Ground,

Firm thru' the fiercest drought and storm.

What heights of love, what depths of peace,

When fears are stilled, when strivings cease!

My Comforter, my All in All,

Here in the love of Christ I stand.[5]

C. H. Spurgeon encouraged his congregation along these lines when he wrote:

It is ever the Holy Spirit's work to turn our eyes away from self to Jesus; but Satan's work is just the opposite of this, for he is constantly trying to make us regard ourselves instead of Christ. He insinuates, "Your sins are too great for pardon; you have no faith; you do not repent enough; you will never be able to continue to the end; you have not the joy of his children; you have such a wavering hold of Jesus." All these are thoughts about self, and we shall never find comfort or assurance by looking within. But the Holy Spirit turns our eyes entirely away from self: he tells us that we are nothing, but that "Christ is all in all." Remember, therefore, it is not your hold of Christ that saves you—it is Christ; it is not your joy in Christ that saves you—it is Christ; it is not even faith in Christ, though that be the instrument—it is Christ's blood and merits; therefore, look not so much to your hand with which you art grasping Christ, as to Christ; look not to your hope, but to Jesus, the source of your hope; look not to your faith, but to Jesus, the author and finisher of your faith. We shall never find happiness by looking at our prayers, our doings, or our feelings; it is what Jesus is, not what we are, that gives rest to the soul. If we would at once overcome Satan and have peace with God, it must be by "looking unto Jesus." Keep your eye simply on him; let his death, his sufferings, his merits, his glories, his intercession, be fresh upon your mind; when you wake in the morning look to him; when your lie down at night look to him. Do not let your hopes or fears come between you and Jesus; follow hard after him, and he will never fail you.[6]

Enough said!

NOTES

PREFACE

1. Ernest Frederick Kevan, *The Grace of Law: A Study in Puritan Theology,* Twin Books Series (Montville, N.J.: Sola Deo Gloria, 1976, 1993), 43.

2. Ibid., 265.

PROLOGUE

1. Neil Postman, *Amusing Ourselves to Death: Public Discourse in the Age of Show Business* (New York: Viking, 1985).

2. John Eldridge, *Wild at Heart: Discovering the Passionate Soul of a Man* (Nashville: Thomas Nelson, 2001).

3. J. I. Packer, *The Collected Shorter Writings of J. I. Packer* (Cumbria, U.K.: Paternoster, 1999), 3:111.

4. John Murray, *Collected Writings of John Murray* (Edinburgh; Carlisle, Pa.: Banner of Truth Trust, 1976), 1:197.

5. Murray, *Collected Writings,* 19.

6. Packer, *Collected Shorter Writings,* 111.

7. Martin Luther, *Commentary on the Epistle to the Galatians* (1535), trans. Theodore Graebner (Grand Rapids: Zondervan, 1949), 131.

8. Charles W. Colson and Nancy Pearcey, *How Now Shall We Live?* (Wheaton, Ill.: Tyndale, 1999), 408.

9. Fred H. Klooster, *Our Only Comfort: A Comprehensive Commentary on the Heidelberg Catechism* (Grand Rapids: Faith Alive Christian Resources, 2001), 1:86.

10. A. R. Vidler, *Christ's Strange Work* (London, 1946), 53, in Ernest Kevan, *The Grace of Law: A Study in Puritan Theology,* Twin Books Series (Nashville, A.J.: Sola Deo Gloria, 1976, 1993), 261.

11. John R. W. Stott, *Romans: God's Good News for the World,* The Bible Speaks Today Series (Downers Grove, Ill.: InterVarsity, 1992; Grand Rapids: Zondervan [distributor], 1994), 192.

12. Samuel Bolton, *The True Bounds of Christian Freedom* (London, Banner of Truth Trust, reprint, 1964), 80; in Kevan, *The Grace of Law,* 165.

13. Donald MacLeod, *A Faith to Live By: Studies in Christian Doctrine* (Montville, N.J.: Christian Focus, 2002), 200.

14. Packer, *Collected Shorter Writings,* 3:116.

15. David Atkinson, *The Message of Ruth: The Wings of Refuge,* The Bible Speaks Today Series (Downers Grove, Ill.: InterVarsity, 1985), 107.

16. Louis Berkhof, *Systematic Theology,* 2d rev. and enl. ed. (Grand Rapids: Eerdmans, 1941). Previously published under the title *Reformed Dogmatics.*

17. MacLeod, *A Faith to Live By,* 194.

18. John Gresham Machen, *The Christian View of Man* (London: Banner of Truth Trust, 1965; Edinburgh; Carlisle, Pa.: Banner of Truth, 1984), 189.

19. Colson, *How Now Shall We Live?* 410.

20. MacLeod, *A Faith to Live By,* 193.

21. Luther, *Galatians,* 129.

22. Machen, *The Christian View of Man,* 195.

23. Luther, *Galatians.*

24. David Wells, *Whatever Happened to the Reformation?* ed. Gary L. W. Johnson and R. Fowler White (Phillipsburg, N.J.: Presbyterian & Reformed, 2001), xxii.

25. Ralph Erskine, *Gospel Sonnets* (1720), in *Works* (Glasgow, 1720, 1778), 10:270, in Kevan, *The Grace of Law,* 261.

26. Bolton, *True Bounds,* in Kevan, *The Grace of Law.*

27. Murray, *Collected Writings,* 204.

28. See also Klooster, *Commentary on the Heidelberg Catechism,* 79.

29. Thomas Taylor, *Regulae Vitae: The Rule of the Law Under the Gospel* (1631), 139–141.

30. MacLeod, *A Faith to Live By,* 195.

31. Samuel Bolton, *The True Bounds of Christian Freedom* (London: Banner of Truth, 1964), 195–96.

32. Samuel Rutherford, *The Trial and Triumph of Faith* (Edinburgh; Carlisle, Pa.: Banner of Truth Trust, 2001), 105, in Kevan, *The Grace of Law,* 247. Originally published as *The Tryal and Triumph of Faith* (London: John Field, 1645; reprinted 1845 by the Committee of the Free Church of Scotland for the Publication of the Works of Scottish Reformers and Divines; this ed. is a reprint of the 1845 ed.).

33. John Owen, *Indwelling Sin in Believers,* vol. 6, *The Works of John Owen,* ed. William H. Goold (reprint of the 1850–53 ed., London: Banner of Truth Trust, 1965–68; Grand Rapids: Baker, 1979), 186.

34. Ezekial Hopkins, *Sermon on John VII.19* (London 1701), in Kevan, *The Grace of Law,* 179.

35. Robert Bolton, *Three-fold Treatise,* "Saints Guide," p. 40; cf. "Selfe-enriching Examination," p. 53, in Kevan, *The Grace of Law,* 221.

36. Luther, *Galatians,* 144.

Hymns:

George Matheson (1842–1906), "Make Me a Captive Lord."

Augustus M. Toplady (1740–1778), "A Debtor to Mercy Alone."

Augustus M. Toplady (1740–1778), "Rock of Ages."

Cecil Frances Alexander (1818–895), "There Is a Green Hill Far Away."

CHAPTER 1: NO OTHER GODS

1. Os Guinness, *Time for Truth: Living Free in a World of Lies, Hype and Spin* (Grand Rapids: Hourglass Books; Baker, 2002).

Hymn:

William Cowper (1731–1800), "O for a Closer Walk with God."

CHAPTER 2: GRAVEN MISTAKES

1. John Owen, *Indwelling Sin in Believers,* vol. 6, *The Works of John Owen,* ed. William H. Goold (reprint of the 1850–53 ed., London: Banner of Truth Trust, 1965–68; Grand Rapids: Baker, 1979).

2. J. Alec Motyer, *Look to the Rock: An Old Testament Background to Our Understanding of Christ* (Leicester, England: Inter-Varsity, 1996), 65.

3. Kwok Pui-Lan, quoted by Susan Cyre, in "Mainline Denial: How Our Churches Are Responding to 'Re-Imagining',", a report on the Re-Imaging conference held in Minneapolis, November 1993. Accessed at http://www.goodnewsmag.org/library/articles/cyre-ma94.htm

4. Motyer, *Look to the Rock,* 134.

5. Motyer, *Look to the Rock.*

6. C. H. Spurgeon, *Morning and Evening: Daily Readings by C. H. Spurgeon,* reading for the morning of June 10. Accessed at a Web site prepared by HEARTLIGHT® Magazine, produced by Heartlight, Inc.: http://www.heartlight.org/spurgeon/.

Hymn:

Frances R. Havergal, 1836–1879, "Take My Life and Let It Be."

CHAPTER 3: WHAT'S IN A NAME?

1. After Ernest C. Reisinger, *Whatever Happened to the Ten Commandments?* (Edinburgh: Banner of Truth, 1999), 9.

2. John Calvin, *John Calvin's Sermons on the Ten Commandments,* ed. and trans., Benjamin W. Farley (Grand Rapids: Baker Book House, 1980), 83.

3. Bruce Milne, *Know the Truth: A Handbook of Christian Belief* (Downers Grove, Ill.: InterVarsity, 1982), 20.

4. Ibid.

5. Derek Prime, *Bible Answers,* (Montville, N.J.: Christian Focus, 2001).

6. J. I. Packer, *Knowing God* (Downers Grove, Ill.: InterVarsity, 1993), 152.

7. John Calvin, *John Calvin's Sermons on the Ten Commandments,* ed. and trans. Benjamin W. Farley (Grand Rapids: Baker Book House, 1980), 950.

8. John Stott, *The Message of the Sermon on the Mount,* The Bible Speaks Today Series (Downers Grove, Ill.: InterVarsity, 1985).

9. Stott, *The Message of the Sermon on the Mount,* 102.

10. J. Alec Motyer, *Look to the Rock: An Old Testament Background to Our Understanding of Christ* (Leicester, England: Inter-Varsity, 1996).

Hymns:

Isaac Watts (1674–1748), "I Sing the Mighty Power of God."

Elizabeth C. Elephane (1830–1869), "Beneath the Cross of Jesus."

John Newton (1725–1807), "How Sweet the Name of Jesus Sounds."

CHAPTER 4: HOLY DAY OR HOLIDAY

1. Adam Wolfson, *The Wall Street Journal,* Thursday, 27 July 2000.

2. Alexis McCrossen, *Holy Day, Holiday: The American Sunday* (Ithaca, N.Y.: Cornell Univ. Press, 2000), 22.

3. Bruce A. Ray, *Celebrating the Sabbath: Finding Rest in a Restless World* (Phillipsburg, N.J.: Presby. & Ref., 2000), 5.

4. John Murray, *Collected Writings of John Murray* (Edinburgh; Carlisle, Pa.: Banner of Truth Trust, 1976), 1:203.

5. Philip Doddridge (1702–51), "My Gracious Lord," adapted.

6. Bruce A. Ray, *Celebrating the Sabbath,* 22.

7. John Murray, *Collected Writings,* 1:223.

8. Joseph A. Pipa, *The Lord's Day* (Montville, N.J.: Christian Focus, 1997), 95.

9. Pipa, *The Lord's Day,* 36.

10. R. T. Beckwith and W. Stott, *The Christian Sunday* (Grand Rapids: Baker, 1978), 30.

11. Derek Prime, *Bible Answers: To Questions about the Christian Faith and Life* (Montville, N.J.: Christian Focus; first published as one book in 2001).

12. Murray, *Collected Writings,* 1:227.

13. Ray, *Celebrating the Sabbath,* 97.

CHAPTER 5: FAMILY LIFE—GOD'S WAY

1. Charles Bridges, *A Commentary on Proverbs* (Edinburgh and Carlisle, Pa.: Banner of Truth Trust; 1846, reprinted 1974 and 1977), 605.

CHAPTER 6: LIFE IS SACRED

1. "District of Columbia Crime Rates 1960–2000," Web site: *The Disaster Center,* "Crime Statistics," accessed at www.disastercenter.com/crime/dccrime.htm.

2. Joan Baez, "The Hitchhickers' Song," © 1970, 1971 Chandros Music (ASCAP).

3. Derek Humphrey, "Prisoner of Conscience: Dr. Jack Kevorkian, Prisoner #284797, Martyr to the cause of the right to choose to die," updated 20 August 2002. Web site: www.finalexit.org/drkframe.html.

4. "Adolescent Suicide: Teenagers Commonly Question the Why and How of Suicide," The Brown University Child and Adolescent Behavior Letter, vol. 14, no. 12, December 1998. Accessed at www.childresearch.net/CYBRARY/NEWS/9812,HTM.

5. "Suicide," U.S. Department of Health and Human Services, Centers for Disease Control and Prevention, data for 2000. Accessed at www.cdc.gov/nchs/fstats/suicide.htm.

6. Similarly, The U.S. Centers for Disease Control and Prevention reported that the reported number of legal abortions in 1997 was 1,186,039; CDC Surveillance Summaries, December 8, 2000. Morbidity and Mortality Weekly Report (MMWR), 2000:49 (no. SS-11; (accessed at www.pregnantpause.org/numbers/abortgen.htm).

7. Derek Prime, Bible Answers: To Questions About the Christian Faith and Life (Montville, N.J.: Christian Focus, 2001), 188.

8. John R. W. Stott, Romans: God's Good News for the World, The Bible Speaks Today Series (Downers Grove, Ill.: InterVarsity, 1992; Grand Rapids: Zondervan [distributor], 1994), 192.

9. C. S. Lewis, "The Humanitarian Theory of Punishment," in God in the Dock: Essays on Theology and Ethics, ed. Walter Hooper (Grand Rapids: Eerdmans, 1970).

CHAPTER 7: YOU SHALL NOT COMMIT ADULTERY

1. Jill Tweedie, The Guardian (London).

2. J. Alec Motyer, Look to the Rock: An Old Testament Background to Our Understanding of Christ (Leicester, England: Inter-Varsity, 1996), 70

3. John Calvin, John Calvin's Sermons on the Ten Commandments, ed. and trans. Benjamin W. Farley (Grand Rapids: Baker, 1980), 170. Readings from this volume are Calvin's sermons on Deuteronomy 4:44–5:3 and Deuteronomy 5:4–7.

4. Motyer, Look to the Rock.

Hymn:

Horatio G. Spafford (1828–1888), "It Is Well with My Soul."

CHAPTER 8: I WAS ONLY BORROWING IT

1. Richard C. Hollinger and Jason L. Davis, 2001 National Retail Security Survey: Final Report, Security Research Project, Department of Sociology and

the Center for Studies in Criminology and Law, Gainesville, Florida, copyright 2002, page 4; www.soc.ufl.edu/srp.htm

2. Derek Prime, *Bible Answers: To Questions About the Christian Faith and Life* (Montville, N.J.: Christian Focus, 2001), 194.

3. Skip Ryan, from a series of sermons preached in December 1977, page 72.

4. Abraham Kuyper, *Calvinism* (Grand Rapids: Eerdmans, 1943). "Calvinism and Politics" lecture.

5. J. Alec Motyer, *Look to the Rock: An Old Testament Background to Our Understanding of Christ* (Leicester, England: Inter-Varsity, 1996).

CHAPTER 9: THE TRUTH MATTERS

1. J. Alec Motyer, *Look to the Rock: An Old Testament Background to Our Understanding of Christ* (Leicester, England: Inter-Varsity, 1996), 135.

2. Motyer, *Look to the Rock,* 134.

3. Derek Prime, *Bible Answers: To Questions About the Christian Faith and Life* (Montville, N.J : Christian Focus, 2001), 196.

4. Charles R. Swindoll, *Killing Giants: Pulling Thorns* (Portland, Oreg.: Multnomah, 1978; Grand Rapids: Zondervan, 1995), 49.

5. Skip Ryan, sermon series on the Ten Commandments.

6. Bryan Chapell, *Holiness by Grace: Delighting in the Joy That Is Our Strength* (Wheaton, Ill.: Crossway, 2001).

Hymns:

Isaac Watts (1674–1748), "When I Survey the Wondrous Cross."

Elisha A. Hoffman (1839–1929), "Leaning on the Everlasting Arms."

CHAPTER 10: THE OTHER MAN'S GRASS

1. "Magnetic Resonance Imaging," Microsoft® Encarta® Online Encyclopedia 2002 at http://encarta.msn.com © 1997-2002, Microsoft Corporation. All rights reserved.

2. James Montgomery Boice, *Foundations of the Faith: A Comprehensive and Readable Theology,* rev. ed., The Master Reference Collection (Downers Grove, Ill.: InterVarsity, 1986), 244.

3. John Calvin, *John Calvin's Sermons on the Ten Commandments,* ed. and trans. Benjamin W. Farley (Grand Rapids: Baker, 1980), 233.

4. Joe Queenan, *Balsamic Dreams* (New York: Picador, 2001), 24.

5. *A Puritan Golden Treasury* (Chicago: Moody, 1975; Banner of Truth Trust, 1977; Puritan, 1989), 68.

6. Derek Prime, *Bible Answers: To Questions About the Christian Faith and Life,* (Montville, N.J.: Christian Focus, 2001), 206.

7. Joe Queenan, *Balsamic Dreams.*

8. Jerome K. Jerome, *Three Men in a Boat* (1889; reprint, London: Penguin, 1957), 26.

9. Sinclair Ferguson, *Tabletalk,* September 1998: 8, 10.

Hymns:

Karolina W. Sandell-Berg (1832–1903), "Day by Day," translated from Swedish to English by Andrew L. Skoog (1856-1934).

Charles Wesley (1708–1788), "Jesus, Lover of My Soul."

Edward Mote (1797–1874), "My Only Hope Is You."

EPILOGUE: GOOD NEWS FOR LAWBREAKERS

1. Jerry Bridges, *The Gospel for Real Life* (Colorado Springs: NavPress, 2002), 53.

2. Stuart Townend, "How Deep the Father's Love for Us," © 1995 Kingsway's Thankyou Music (Admin. By EMI Christian Music Publishing). All rights reserved. International copyright secured. CCLI song #1558110.

3. Jerry Bridges, *The Gospel for Real Life,* 103.

4. Benjamin B. Warfield, *The Works of Benjamin B. Warfield* (Grand Rapids: Baker, 1931; reprint, 1991), 7:113.

5. Stuart Townend and Keith Getty, "In Christ Alone," © 2001 Kingsway's Thankyou Music/MCPS. All rights reserved. International copyright secured. CCLI song #3350395.

6. C. H. Spurgeon, *Morning and Evening: Daily Readings by C. H. Spurgeon,* reading for the morning of June 28. Accessed at a Web site prepared by HEARTLIGHT® Magazine, produced by Heartlight, Inc.: http://www.heartlight.org/spurgeon/

Hymns:

Charlotte Elliott (1789-1871), "Just As I Am, Without One Plea."

TRUTH FOR LIFE®

THE BIBLE-TEACHING MINISTRY OF **ALISTAIR BEGG**

At Truth For Life, our mission is to teach the Bible with clarity and relevance so that unbelievers will be converted, believers will be established, and local churches will be strengthened.

Since 1995, Truth For Life has aired a Bible-teaching program on the radio, which is now distributed on 1,590 radio outlets each day, and freely on podcast and on the Truth For Life mobile app. Additionally, a large content archive of full-length Bible-teaching sermons is available for free download at www.truthforlife.org.

Truth For Life also makes full-length Bible-teaching available on CD and DVD. These materials, and also books authored by Alistair Begg, are made available at cost, with no markup, so that price is not a barrier to those seeking a deeper understanding of God's Word.

The ministry connects with listeners at live listener and pastor events and conferences across the U.S. and Canada in cities where the radio program is heard.

CONTACT TRUTH FOR LIFE

In the U.S.:

PO Box 398000, Cleveland, OH 44139 1.888.588.7884
www.truthforlife.org   letters@truthforlife.org

In Canada:

P.O. Box 19008, Delta, BC V4L 2P8   1.877.518.7884
www.truthforlife.ca   letters@truthforlife.ca

And also at:

www.facebook.com/truthforlife   www.twitter.com/truthforlife

MOODY Radio™

*From the Word **to Life***

Moody Radio produces and delivers compelling programs filled with biblical insights and creative expressions of faith that help you take the next step in your relationship with Christ.

You can hear Moody Radio on 36 stations and more than 1,500 radio outlets across the U.S. and Canada. Or listen on your smartphone with the Moody Radio app!

www.moodyradio.org